Rebellion and Reconciliation

THE WILLIAMSBURG DECORATIVE ARTS SERIES

GRAHAM HOOD, *Editor*

Rebellion and Reconciliation

SATIRICAL PRINTS ON THE REVOLUTION AT WILLIAMSBURG

By Joan D. Dolmetsch

Published by

THE COLONIAL WILLIAMSBURG FOUNDATION • *Williamsburg, Virginia*

Distributed by THE UNIVERSITY PRESS OF VIRGINIA • *Charlottesville, Virginia*

LIBRARY OF CONGRESS CATALOGING IN PUBLICATION DATA
Colonial Williamsburg Foundation.
    Rebellion and reconciliation.
    (The Williamsburg decorative arts series)
    Bibliography: p. 215
    Includes index.
    1. United States—History—Revolution, 1775-1783—Humor, cari-
catures, etc.—Exhibitions. I. Dolmetsch, Joan D. II. Title. III. Title:
Satirical prints on the Revolution at Williamsburg. IV. Series.
E298.C64 1976   973.3'02'07   75-41443
ISBN 0-87935-032-6 (Colonial Williamsburg)
ISBN 0-8139-0682-2 (Univ. Press of Va.)

PRINTED IN THE UNITED STATES OF AMERICA

CONTENTS

FOREWORD

POLITICAL satires—or as modern parlance has it, political cartoons—have a long and vigorous history. Even today they show no symptoms of decay, our present surfeit of pictorial images (both moving and still) notwithstanding. Recent political traumas in this country, for example, gave rise to memorable cartoons that may well, in two hundred years' time, produce just as dramatic an impact as anything written.

That the painful wrenching away of the American colonies from the British Empire should have produced some equally memorable images is not surprising, considering the cataclysmic nature of the events and the fact that the cartoon or satire suffered no competition, as commentary, from the camera. Then, as now, the most pungent images were often those that depicted a meteoric fall from grace, proffered an easy scapegoat, or came out trenchantly on the side of the underdog. The latter, of course, were manna to the colonists, who admired and emulated them.

It may surprise some of us that the colonists' cause found such expressive and tenacious exponents in England. Freedom was not only fought for in this country with weapons, but also in London with words and gestures. For this reason we feel that this selection from our collections of English and American eighteenth-century prints makes an appropriate bicentennial offering.

Most of these satires were acquired during the great expansion of the Colonial Williamsburg collections under the curatorship of John M. Graham II. The nucleus of the collection of political satires came from the collection of H. Dunscombe Colt, acquired in 1960. They form a superb and graphic pedagogic resource, helping to amplify the larger messages of Colonial Williamsburg. For this, as well as an able exposition of some of the more recondite aspects of the prints themselves, Joan Dolmetsch's account will serve as a model and will amply repay the reading.

GRAHAM HOOD
Director of Collections

viii

INTRODUCTION

READERS of today's newspapers and magazines are thoroughly familiar with cartoons—pictures drawn to accompany a written commentary, and generally sarcastic, humorous, or prophetic in content. While most cartoons pertain to major news events, some simply comment on a local issue or are devoted to a new social fad or custom. Whatever the subject, the intent is to sway the reader's opinion toward that of the commentator.

In the eighteenth century such illustrations were known as satires or caricatures, terms whose meanings encompassed grotesque or ludicrous representations of persons or situations achieved through exaggeration, ridicule, or denunciation. The earliest satires were written descriptions only, and the addition or transfer of meaning to pictorial art came gradually. The use of the word *cartoon* to denote such a depiction did not gain popular acceptance until the mid-nineteenth century, its prior usage being confined to the artistic sense: a design, sketch, or preliminary drawing for a subject such as a fresco or tapestry. (See No. 35 for a rare exception to this usage.)

Few early satires employed the humorous slant so often found in cartoons today. Most frequently they were serious condemnations of political or religious situations and of the leaders responsible. Effective use of satire was made by Martin Luther during the Reformation when, under his direction, traditional religious symbols were turned into objects of scorn.[1] Some of those inventions—renderings of papal supporters surrounded by whores, the pope as Devil, the scale, balance, or wheel of fate, the open pit of Hell—are still in use today. Luther's enemies created equally vicious symbolism using whole or parts of animals and mythological creatures to express their contempt for their foes.

The past and present history of satire clearly demonstrates that the more serious the event, the more brilliantly conceived the depiction seems to be. In the seventeenth century, England, torn by the strife of the Civil War, saw a burgeoning of the satire. Native designers not only created their own styles but were also quick to borrow ideas from talented foreign satirists such as the Dutch. The results were often so libelous or even treasonous in nature that political and religious leaders sought to suppress them. Many makers worked under commission for publishers and preferred to remain anonymous or resorted to satirical pseudonyms. Publishers were not easily intimidated and, although under constant threat of punishment, continued to issue satires. No accurate records survive of how many satires might have been printed or sold—or even how many of any individual item—but diaries, letters, and other documents of the period do mention individual successes or failures.[2]

In England the first significant eighteenth-century event to elicit the satirist's response was the collapse of the South Sea Bubble and its French equivalent, John Law's Mississippi scheme. Both countries were experiencing severe economic difficulties and financiers devised grandiose schemes to rescue the nations from imminent disaster—and incidentally to make investors wealthy overnight. The failure of the ventures stimulated some of the sharpest and most humorous satires ever created on either side of the English Channel. Among those who found the subject worthy of pictorial comment was the young William Hogarth, just venturing into the field of printmaking. His satire *The South Sea Scheme* appeared in 1721.[3]

To discover the real beginning of the Revolutionary War satires pictured here one must first examine those concerned with two mid-eighteenth-century conflicts, the War of the Austrian Succession and the French and Indian War (Seven Years' War). Once the potential wealth of America and the Far East was fully realized, European nations struggled for control of these new sources of income. Disputes erupted as nations vied for the strategic ports and fortresses necessary to command the seas and provide easy access to trade routes.

In 1740 the War of the Austrian Succession broke out on the Continent as nations fought for portions of the vast Hapsburg domain. When Britain joined Austria and Sardinia in an effort to remove France and Spain from Italy, the war intensified and spread into America where France and England became engaged in the conflict now known as King George's War. Peace eventually was restored by a conference held in 1748 at Aix-la-Chapelle, but the resulting treaty did little to settle territorial disputes.

Within six years another and larger conflict broke out, known on the American continent as the French and Indian War, and in Europe as the Seven Years' War. Disagreement between France and England over control of the strategically important Canadian areas from the St. Lawrence River to the Great Lakes eventually expanded into open warfare involving boundaries in almost all of colonial America from the Atlantic Ocean west to the Mississippi River and south to Virginia. As bitter fighting continued on land and sea, the colonies joined their mother country. When the war spread to Europe in 1756, Prussia allied itself with Britain, Austria with France. Spain entered the dispute and lost important territories to England.[4] Finally in 1763 the warring nations met in Paris to reach an accord that in turn opened the way for the colonies to seek independence.

The agreement left England and Spain as sole occupants of the American continent north of Mexico. Defeated and humiliated, many of her colonial possessions gone, France was anxious for revenge. England, although victorious, was confronted by new problems, not the least of which was the financial crisis resulting from the heavy expenditures necessary to fight two wars in so short a period.

In an effort to cope with the mounting fiscal crisis, George Grenville, the British chancellor of the Exchequer, presented to the House of Commons in 1764 a budget that included provisions for a number of taxes to be levied on and in the colonies. American opposition was swift and positive.

Events from 1764 to the end of the Revolution moved with such rapidity that satirists were seldom without new controversies to challenge their wits. No person, no event escaped their notice. Symbolic representations of countries and leaders, some derived from long familiar themes, took shape, and many remained in use throughout the Revolution. Makers also sought new motifs and ventured into the realms of literature, art, theater, and even history itself to find more vivid imagery to represent the struggle.

Even as artists sought new designs for satires, so too did they alter their techniques for making them. Satires are topical in nature, so speed in designing and publishing them is essential. By the mid-eighteenth century most makers were ready to forsake the more conventional and cumbersome technique of line engraving for the less time-consuming etching process. Woodcuts were seldom used during this period except for newspaper cuts. Subsequent hand-coloring of the satires was also reduced, and those that were colored display the haste with which the paint was applied.

Any attempt to assess the artistic merits of these simple prints is difficult. In fact, to apply the term "artistic" to satires is probably a misuse of the word, for to most this suggests some form of beauty, and there is truly nothing beautiful about such works. Throughout the eighteenth century most of the satires were crudely conceived by anonymous makers, many of whom were barely more than inexpert craftsmen hired by a publisher to translate his political ideas onto a plate for printing.[5] The use of the term artist to designate these people is eschewed in this volume and satirist, designer, or simply maker has been substituted. Only a few satires can be attributed to artists of any note, and their skill in translating ideas into print is obvious.

As one views the satires in this volume, he will find that it is often the less complex work that has the greatest impact, while those that attempt to combine a number of messages within a single plate quickly lose their effect in the plethora of detail. Excellent examples of forceful satires may be found in *America in Flames* (No. 30), which pictures the closing of the port of Boston, or the cover design of the reconciliation between Britain and America, which with a few sketched figures presents the viewer with a precise account of changes in alliances. Conversely, the Dutch satires that begin at No. 62 are so complicated in design that it is often difficult to understand their message.

How effective this pictorial propaganda was during the Revolutionary period is difficult to determine. Certainly satires appeared with great frequency at a time when there was little other visual material to influence the public. It is doubtful that a successful printmaker such as Matthew Darly, who published over three hundred satires during the period 1771–81 (of which about one-third can be classified as political in nature), would have continued to issue them had they not been well received.

The collecting of political satires at Colonial Williamsburg began in the early years of the restoration, not only because of the historical importance of the prints, but also because evidence exists that our ancestors owned such works. The Purdie and Dixon *Virginia Gazette* of October 17, 1766, carried the following advertisement:

> TO BE SOLD,
> *By the Subscriber in* NORTHUMBERLAND, A CURIOUS collection of Prints and PAMPHLETS relating to all the transactions in *Europe* for some years past, containing about 200 prints, or pictures, representing all the persons and characters of note in *Europe*, viz. Crowned Heads, Ministers of State, Politicians, Patriots, Admirals, Generals &c. &c. in a very striking, expressive, and historical light, with their proper characters, schemes, &c. in the hieroglyphick or caricatura manner, with the most severe and entertaining satires on some, and the greatest applause to others. There are about forty pamphlets of prose and verse on both sides of the question, by CHURCHILL, &c. The purchaser shall have them at 50 percent, advance on the first cost.
>
> JOSEPH McADAM

In 1960 the Foundation acquired, virtually complete, a large collection of satires from the estate of H. Dunscombe Colt. As a result of his long friendship with R. T. H. Halsey, one of the twentieth century's most avid collectors of Americana including political satires,

Mr. Colt also became interested in them.[6] While his collection never achieved the size of Halsey's, Colt was able to duplicate most of the important Revolutionary pieces and succeeded in acquiring a few that escaped his friend's notice. Colt also broadened the scope of his holdings to include materials concerned with England's internal problems, many of which were influenced by the colonial dispute.

It should be pointed out that although most of the American Revolutionary satires in the Colonial Williamsburg collection are of English origin, other countries did produce similar works. Included are a group made in Holland about 1780 (Nos. 62–73). They are not unlike those produced in England; many of the same allegorical and symbolic representations appear and most are procolonial in content. Although restrictive in subject matter, the Dutch artists were generally more expansive in style. Meticulous care was given to small details in both the central theme and background material.

Many of the satires made in England and on the Continent were sympathetic to the colonial cause and were, of course, widely popular and often copied on these shores. Of the small number of printmakers in America, few had either the time or the inclination to compete. There were, however, such notable exceptions as Benjamin Franklin and Paul Revere.

Describing eighteenth-century political satire has been greatly simplified by the British Museum's eleven-volume catalog in which both political and personal satires from the period 1620 to 1832 have been carefully analyzed.[7] Mary Dorothy George was responsible for categorizing the Revolutionary War period that included many of the satires in this volume. In other books and articles Mrs. George expanded on the subject, and her contributions to the general study of eighteenth-century prints are invaluable to anyone interested in the field.[8]

For some readers, this volume may provide their first encounter with eighteenth-century satires, and therefore a close analysis of one work may prove helpful here. Details may easily escape the viewer unless he has some idea of what to anticipate because only the

Boston cannonaded.

Boston Port Bill.

Military Law.

BOSTON Petition.

The able Doctor, or America Swallowing the Bitter Draught.

B. M. 5226
London Magazine, May 1, 1774

1960-45

7

broad implications of the print are discussed in the catalog entries. In most instances the historic event that inspired the print will be as familiar as the story of the Boston Tea Party, which provoked one of the most popular of all Revolutionary satires, *The able Doctor, or America Swallowing the Bitter Draught* (See preceding page.)[9]

As a means of bolstering the sagging English economy, the British ministry deemed it necessary to impose a duty on colonial importation of tea, a commodity that was very popular in America. When three ships carrying the heavily taxed cargo reached Boston, the colonists would not allow the goods to be unloaded, and the royal governor, Thomas Hutchinson, responded by refusing to permit the vessels to leave. If the duty were not paid within twenty days the governor could confiscate the tea and profit personally from it. Incensed by these events, a group of patriots disguised as Indians boarded the ships and threw the tea into the harbor. In retaliation for the destruction, the ministry ordered the port of Boston closed.

The tea party occurred on December 16, 1773. The print first appeared in the *London Magazine* for May 1774 and was copied by Paul Revere for the June issue of the *Royal American Magazine*. The English designer displays a procolonial or antigovernment bias then held by some of the British.

For purposes of satire, America's unfortunate position is symbolized by a partially robed female Indian who has been forced to the ground by her enemies. Lord Mansfield, wearing robes appropriate to his position as lord chief justice, displays his firm belief in England's foreign policy by holding down America's arms. Lord Sandwich, in charge of the British navy, clasps her legs together with one hand, while using the other to lift her robe and lewdly peer beneath it. The prime minister, Lord North, pours hot tea down America's throat, but she regurgitates it back in his face. A paper in North's pocket is labeled "Boston Port Bill." Appropriately attired to represent France and Spain, two figures watch the scene, their gestures suggesting concern for the unhappy female. The figure of Britannia turns away and covers her eyes with her hands, reluctant to be a witness to the schemes of her ministers. Lord Bute, most often pictured in these satires in his native Scottish dress, stands with a drawn sword representing "Military law." Bute had been one of the king's most influential advisers, and although by 1773 he was no longer in public office, many people believed that he still strongly influenced government policy. In the foreground is a torn piece of paper—"Boston Petition"—signifying Boston's protest against the port closing, while on the horizon, symbolic of the blockade, the harbor is pictured "cannonaded."

The British political leaders depicted in this satire will appear often in the prints that follow, as will others who were equally responsible for government policies before and during the war. Caricatures of facial features or gestures, nicknames, or native attire were often employed to emphasize their identity. An excellent example of this is the characterization often used for Lord Sandwich, one of the ministers directly blamed for many of the anticolonial policies just previous to the Revolution. He is often satirized by the nickname and in the guise of "Jemmy Twitcher," one of Captain MacHeath's highwaymen in John Gay's *The Beggar's Opera.* The work was first performed in 1728 and became a great favorite with Londoners. The symbolic transfer of one of its roguish characters to a public figure generally believed to possess many of the same traits would have been well understood by purchasers of satiric prints.

Nations received similar symbolic treatment. Britain was most often a female until just before the end of the war, when the John Bull character became a fashionable substitute. The English shield and often the British lion formed a part of her imagery. America usually appeared as an Indian, more often female than male, although occasionally the figure of a "Yankee Doodle Dandy" complete with feather in his hat was substituted after about 1776.[10]

The shoreline became an obvious setting for designers who wished to comment on the international scope of the conflict. However, since England and its government were regarded as the prime culprits, the principal action usually places them in the foreground with America shown across the water.

While not every Colonial Williamsburg political satire is included in this volume, all of the most significant Revolutionary ones are depicted. The satires are arranged in chronological order to enable the reader to trace their development through this crucial historic period. When the print is listed in the British Museum catalog, the appropriate entry number has been provided so that those wishing more detailed information may begin their study there. A selective bibliography of readily available books is included at the end.[11] Many of them provide more historical information on the period and a majority include additional illustrations of these fascinating historical documents.

I am indebted to a number of people who have made this book possible. Special thanks are due John Graham, retired director of collections, and Edward M. Riley, director of research at Colonial Williamsburg, for fostering and supporting my early interest and research on the Colt collection. I would also like to thank the staff of the Colonial Williamsburg Foundation, particularly Graham Hood, director of collections, who saw the potential of these historical documents and encouraged their publication, and Susan Gibson, librarian for collections. Wilson Duprey, former curator of prints and Wendy J. Shadwell, present curator of prints at the New-York Historical Society, and Elizabeth Roth, curator of prints at the New York Public Library, offered advice and help on my study trips to New York. Professor John C. Riely, Yale University, read the manuscript and offered many helpful suggestions. My husband, Professor Carl R. Dolmetsch, was always present in the background to help pin down elusive literary allusions and to generally bolster my spirits during the writing of the book.

NOTES

1. An excellent and detailed discussion of early satires may be found in the introduction and first three chapters of M. Dorothy George, *English Political Caricature: A Study of Opinion and Propaganda*. Vol. 1: *to 1792*. Vol. 2: *1793-1832* (Oxford, 1959).

2. For more information on early publishers and publications see Herbert M. Atherton, *Political Prints in the Age of Hogarth: A Study of the Ideographic Representation of Politics* (Oxford, 1974).

3. Hogarth's ability to translate social and moral problems into pictorial images, most often satiric in nature, was important. However, although his influence is reflected in the work of other satirists

throughout the century, Hogarth only occasionally designed pieces that were purely political in content. For a discussion and appraisal of Hogarth's contributions to the artistic life of the eighteenth century see Ronald Paulson, *Hogarth: His Life, Art, and Times,* 2 vols. (New Haven, Conn., 1971).

4. During this phase of the war Spain lost Martinique, St. Lucia, Grenada, Havana, and Manila.

5. In 1735 Hogarth was instrumental in pressuring Parliament to pass a copyright law that protected printmakers from plagiarism by allowing them to register their works. Many eighteenth-century graphics made after 1735 carry a statement of rights, which generally appears just under the publisher's name, although for obvious reasons few political satirists availed themselves of this protection.

6. Halsey wrote *The Boston Port Bill as Pictured by a Contemporary London Cartoonist* for the Grolier Club of New York in 1904. In 1939 he mounted an exhibit of "Impolitical Prints" for the New York Public Library that was described and cataloged in *Bulletin of the New York Public Library,* 45 (November 1939): 795-829.

7. *Catalogue of Prints and Drawings in the British Museum.* Division I: *Political and Personal Satires,* prepared by Edward Hawkins, Vols. 1-4, 1870-83. The title of Vols. 5-11, 1935-54, prepared by Mary Dorothy George, was changed to *Catalogue of Political and Personal Satires Preserved in the Department of Prints and Drawings in the British Museum.*

8. George, *English Political Caricature,* is of particular importance in the field of political satire.

9. The bicentennial celebration has done much to renew interest in the history and leaders of the Revolutionary War. For readers desiring to refresh their minds quickly on certain key events, Mark Mayo Boatner III, *Encyclopedia of the American Revolution* (New York, 1966), is most helpful.

10. There is no way to precisely date or document the event that caused "Yankee Doodle Dandy," most often pictured as a shabbily dressed soldier, but always with a jaunty feather stuck in his hat, to become a symbol for America. The idea, however, was no doubt suggested by the English "Macaronis," who included feathers in or at the top of their elaborately dressed coiffeurs. The general style was known in New England as early as December 31, 1753, when Peter Burn advertised "Two White Hair Wigs with feather tops in the newest taste at London" in the *Boston Evening Post.* For additional information on the English Macaroni see Joan Dolmetsch, "A New Look at the Old Mod," *Antiques,* 92 (December 1967): 854-57.

11. So many books and catalogs are appearing during America's bicentennial celebration that it is impossible to list all of them that might contain pertinent information. Emphasis has therefore been placed on general works that are illustrated profusely.

Rebellion and Reconciliation

THE EUROPEAN STATE JOCKIES
Running a Heat for the BALLANCE OF POWER,
with various designs adapted for the Year 1740.
Invented by the President of the Political Society, & Inscribed to the Members thereof.
Published according to Act of Parliament 28 March 1740.

AUT MORS AUT VICTORIA

QUATUOR MARIA VINDICO
CUBA I.

America

1. *THE EUROPEAN STATE JOCKIES, RUNNING A HEAT FOR THE BALLANCE OF POWER.*

DATE: March 25, 1740
SIZE: 11½″ x 15¼″ (29.2 cm. x 38.7 cm.)

THE first in a series of political satires commenting on the "race" then taking place among European nations for domination of newly discovered, explored, and potentially wealthy lands across the seas appeared in London shops in 1737. In addition to vividly picturing this struggle, the satires commented on many of the domestic problems then facing the individual countries. All in the series were exceedingly complex in design and used for their setting a seashore populated with a combination of human and allegorical figures. *The European State Jockies*, published in 1740, was the fourth and last of the group.

Among the more important elements in the print is the platform which is placed at the upper right, serving to support on the left end a balance. Symbols of "Mediation" and "Convention" rest in one pan, and in the other representations of the ruling forces: bribery, church (cardinal's hat), and political leaders (animal heads). Seated right on the platform are America and Africa united for freedom, while on the left Europe and Asia look to each other for trade protection.

Other international struggles are presented in the foreground. To the right Britannia claims victory over France in the Cuban dispute, while in the center Russia rides a bear which is celebrating defeat of elephant Turkey by kicking it in the rear. To the left a hog burdened with merchandise and held by its master Holland decides to drop out of the race at mid-post. On the left the Devil acting on behalf of France leads a group of cardinals to the conclave which, after a long and acrimonious session, elected the French candidate as Pope Benedict XIV.[1]

In the background English ships sail off across the ocean toward America. The Spanish fleet is blockaded in the port of Cadiz, cut off from the lucrative trade in the Spanish-American colonies.

As confrontations between the European nations increased, the complex satires commenting on large numbers of problems would become fewer, being replaced by works simpler in design that depicted single events. However, many of the allegorical representations utilized in this work would become permanent and would be repeated in future satires.

B.M. 2449   1960-30

1. The power of the pope at this period was equivalent to that of a head of state.

2. *THE CONGRESS OF THE BRUTES.*

DATE: About 1748
SIZE: 9¾″ x 13¾″ (24.8 cm. x 34.9 cm.)

IN 1748 leaders of the major European powers met in Aix-la-Chapelle to discuss a peace treaty ending a conflict that had involved not only the Continent but colonial America as well. The ensuing agreement would have far-reaching consequences, for in redistributing desirable territories the stage was actually set for more disputes, culminating in the American Revolution. By using animals to symbolize the countries at the meeting, the unknown designer of this satire presents a humorous comment on the proceedings.

From a perch on the back of a chair to the right, the French cock, holding in a claw the proposed treaty, seems to dominate the group.[1] Peering through spectacles, a neutral ape examines the document. The dog on the left, Genoa, is forced to part with a portion of its territory, then referred to as the Marquisate of Final, to Sardinia, but has other territorial losses restored. Lion England unhappily surrenders Cape Breton Island to France. The Austrian eagle laments giving up three duchies, Prussia, Silesia, and Glatz, as the griffin representing Silesia requests only remembrance. The Spanish leopard desires a number of territories, including Gibraltar, and receives three, which do not include the latter. Prussia, a demanding wolf, insists on Silesia, and Holland, the boar, claims a new, good, but unspecified barrier.

B.M. 3009   1960-146

---

1. The animals used to symbolize the nations had become traditional by mid-century; most are still in use today.

The CONGRESS of the BRUTES.

3. *BRITAIN'S RIGHTS MAINTAIND: OR FRENCH AMBITION DISMANTLED.*

MAKER: Louis Peter Boitard
DATE: August 11, 1755
SIZE: 8¾" x 12⅞" (22.2 cm. x 32.8 cm.)

BY 1755 the bitter disputes between England and France over control of North American landholdings erupted into open fighting which became known as the French and Indian War. Louis Boitard, one of a group of French engravers working in London at the time, seized the opportunity to design a number of satires that were pro-English in sentiment. In *Britain's Rights maintaind* he combines allegorical animals with mythological and human figures to comment on the conflict in general and on a naval engagement between fleets of the two warring nations that actually did not take place because a heavy fog enshrouded the planned area of confrontation.

Female Britannia holding a pole with a liberty cap entreats Mars and Neptune, representing the English populace, to maintain their rights and be brave.[1] At her side the British lion threatens the cock as it plucks out feathers labeled with the names of French areas coveted by the English. With his sword Mars cuts through the robes of France on which is a map of North America. He promises honor for the British. His companion Neptune, using his trident in a similar threatening manner, swears equal allegiance to the cause. France is also represented by a robed female figure who laments that heretics will now possess some of her land. Representing French politicians, a fop blames much of his country's disasters on the French fleet that became lost in the fog. Jack Tar, the typical English seaman, tells the fop that now the rightful owner has assumed possession of North America. Standing in front of Mars is a small Indian boy, America, taunting the cock by inquiring how it will get home without its feathers.

Boitard has added another satiric element to the design by placing a column celebrating George II's victories in the background. Around this pillar surmounted by the English royal arms dance a group of elated citizens and sailors.

B.M. 3331   1960-31

---

1. Britain is depicted as a female in most of the satires until about 1780 when a bull or another more rugged figure appears.

BRITAIN's RIGHTS maintaind; or FRENCH AMBITION dismantled.

Addrest to the Laudable Societys of ANTI-GALICANS, The generous Promoters of British Arts & Manufactories

By their most Sincere Well wisher and truly devoted Humble Servant   A Lover of his Country

4. *BRITISH RESENTMENT OR THE FRENCH FAIRLY COOPT AT LOUISBOURG:*

MAKERS: Louis Peter Boitard, designer; John June, engraver.
PUBLISHER: Thomas Bowles, and John Bowles and Son.
DATE: September 25, 1755
SIZE: 11¾″ x 16¾″ (29.8 cm. x 42.5 cm.)

ONE of the most famous of Louis Boitard's satires on the French and Indian War is this work that appeared in September 1755, just three months after the French fort at Louisbourg was successfully blockaded by the English. As in the previous satire, Boitard here uses a combination of real and mythological figures to comment on the event. However, in addition to using descriptive material within the design he has added a series of reference numbers that form a legend at the bottom further elucidating the print.

At number 1 Britannia seated on her throne is intent on offering the Americans protection in the form of Neptune and Mars, the symbolic gods of war, who appear at number 2. The British lion, 3, paws a map delineating the areas to which he lays claim—Ohio, Virginia, and Nova Scotia. At number 4 a British sailor, 5, views the eclipse of France by England and points it out to an obviously distressed Frenchman. Yet another English sailor, 6, has the French cock by the throat causing it to disgorge forts formerly under French dominion but now claimed by the British. Another Frenchman, 7, shows alarm at the situation and looks down at number 8 where the English rose blooms as the French lily dies. Number 9, a cage in which Frenchmen are imprisoned, is a symbolic motif that will appear again at satire No. 28 in this volume, where it will depict the similar plight of the Bostonians during the American Revolution. A Frenchman in a canoe at 10 is swept over Niagara Falls, and at 11 a cannon labeled as Oliver Cromwell's device for putting down rebellions is aimed toward the French. Number 12 represents the monument erected in 1755 to mark the beginning of open hostilities between the French and British. Several small naval skirmishes between the two countries culminated on June 10 of that year when Capt. William Howe succeeded in capturing two French vessels.

B.M. 3332   1960-32

BRITISH RESENTMENT or the FRENCH fairly COOPT at Louisbourg.

I. Boitard Invt et Delin.

Publish'd according to Act of Parliament 25 Sepr 1755.

J. June Sculp

1 Britannia attending to the complaints of her injur'd Americans, receives them into her protection. 2 Neptune & Mars unite in their defence
3 The British Lion keeping his dominions under his paw, safe from invaders. 4 The British Arms eclipsing those of France. 5 A British
Sailor pointing to the eclipse, & leering at a French Politician trapt by his own Schemes. 6 An English Saylor encouraged by a Soldier, Squeezes
the Gallic Cock by the throat, & makes him disgorge the French usurpations in America. 7 A French Political Schemer beholds the operation with
grief and Confusion. 8 The English Rose erect, the French Lilly drooping. 9 A Gang of brave Saylors exulting at the Starving French coopt up
10 The French overset at the fall of Niagara. 11 Cromwells device. 12 A Monument due to real Merit.

Printed for J. Bowles in St. Pauls Church Yard, & Ino. Bowles & Son, in Cornhil.

5. *THE ENGLISH LION DISMEMBER'D*

DATE: [1756]
SIZE: 9½" x 13¼" (24.1 cm. x 33.7 cm.)

IN 1756, the date of this satire, England found itself in grave trouble on many foreign fronts. War against the French, which actually had been in progress for almost two years, was now formally declared. The Mediterranean island of Minorca had fallen to France. The generally optimistic view of British supremacy depicted in the previous two satires is replaced by calls from angry and frustrated leaders for explanations of defeats. Except for the British lion and the French cock all figures in the drawing are now human.[1]

The lion and cock occupy the middle foreground. The lion's paws represent Nova Scotia and Oswego, areas presently in danger; Minorca has already been severed. Standing on the British flag, the cock declares that he will tear it to pieces. Two Frenchman watching the scene declare that the lion will lose more paws. On the right the lord mayor of London and aldermen ask two returning messengers why Minorca has been lost; they are told that it was because of poor political planning. Behind the lion a group of Hanoverian soldiers announce that they have come to keep England alive, but dubious English countrymen standing nearby refuse their aid, commenting that they believe the Germans to be more interested in whores, cards, hunting, and horseracing than in commerce and glory.

To the left officials are meeting to ascertain why Admiral Byng, in charge of the Minorca campaign, was unsuccessful. Byng points to the battle plan hanging on the wall that has the following description:

> B . . g's Plea.
> With thirteen Ships to twelve says B--g
> It were a shame to meet 'em
> And then with twelve to twelve a thing
> Impossible to beat 'em
> When more to many less to few
> And even still not right
> Arithmetic will plainly shew
> 'T were wrong in B--g to fight.

B.M. 3547   1960-33

---

1. Although animals or portions of animals, particularly heads, continue to appear in satires, they will be seen less frequently during the Revolutionary period as the designers strive for more realistic depictions of politicians and settings.

THE ENGLISH LION DISMEMBER'D

Or the Voice of the Public for an enquiry into the loss of Minorca – with Ad.^l Bing's plea before his Examiners.

Publish'd according to Act of Parliament.   Sold by the Printsellers of London & Westminster.

6. *A NURSE FOR THE HESS--NS.*

DATE: About 1756
SIZE: 6¼" x 11⅞" (15.9 cm. x 30.2 cm.)

A CONTINUING debate raged in England concerning the staffing of the army with Hessian soldiers, payment for whom was very expensive.

This satire offers an interesting exception to the somewhat more standardized outdoor settings generally preferred by eighteenth-century satirists and instead places the action within a house. A modestly furnished room is pictured, probably a kitchen judging by the large fireplace and accessories. A nurse rocks a large cradle in which rest a Hessian soldier and his horse. Another soldier warms himself in front of the roaring fire. The nurse, representing the ministry, wears a cap proclaiming that she has been hired for four years, which refers to the period that the Hessian mercenaries agreed to serve. Her charges wear belts enumerating the financial cost of their stay. The soldiers outside busily load and carry away sacks of money, payment for their services.

A lullaby printed beneath the picture vividly describes the situation further:

Nurse.   Lulla—by Baby Bunting!
              Why come you here a hunting?

Hess—n. To taak care of Honey,
              And Fatten vid Your Money.

Nurse.   Lulla-by Baby Bunting!
              When will you leave off hunting?

Hess—n. Ven You can geef no more e,
              And be, like de Hess—ns poore e.

B.M. 3478   1960-62

24

Nurſe.— Lulla-by Baby Bunting!
      Why come you here a hunting?
Heſſ-n.— To taak care of Honey,
      And fatten vid Your Money.

Nurſe.— Lulla-by Baby Bunting!
      When will you leave off hunting?
Heſſ-n.— Ven You can geef no more e,
      And be like de Heſſ-ns poore e.

Sold in May's Buildings Covent Garden—wh'is 50 more

7. *THE RECRUITING SERJEANT OR BRITTANNIAIS HAPPY PROSPECT.*

MAKER: LEONARDO.DA.VINCI[1]
DATE: [1757]
SIZE: 7¾" x 13¾" (19.7 cm. x 34.9 cm.)

GEORGE TOWNSHEND, older brother of Charles the politician, is believed to have been the artist responsible for this satire. His abilities as a caricaturist were well known and admired by important English politicians of the period.[2] At the time, 1757, Henry Fox was attempting to form a new government. The problem of recruiting an army, commented on in the previous satire, was still present, and in fact that controversy had contributed to the fall of the previous ministry.

Townshend makes skillful use of figures, one with an animal head as vehicles for his satire. A group of five approach a small temple that houses the statue of a very fat duke of Cumberland. The base of the pedestal, inscribed in Latin, declares that England will triumph over all. The first in line is Fox, who calls for volunteers to serve in the military government. Next is Welbore Ellis, an agent of Fox and vice-treasurer of Ireland, a potential source of recruits. Carrying a cricket bat and knapsack, the earl of

Sandwich follows, declaring his delight in such political games. The short, rotund figure represents Bubb Doddington, who proclaims dislike of Fox's proposals. Last in line, with his back to the viewer, is the earl of Winchelsea, who would turn out all of the mercenaries. To the rear, supposedly carrying the Hessians back home, a number of ships are shown in full sail.

The discussion and disagreement as to how England could best obtain fighting forces from outside and thus save its own populace from such trials would continue to trouble the country for many years and would provide much material for future satires.

B.M. 3581   1960-34

---

1. This obviously fictitious name is picked out in dotted letters on the Colonial Williamsburg impression; it does not appear on the British Museum copy.

2. M. Dorothy George, *English Political Caricature to 1792* (Oxford, 1959), pp. 101—2, 105.

8. *UNTITLED*

MAKER: I. Miller
PUBLISHED: *London Magazine*
DATE: 1758
SIZE: 8″ x 4¾″ (20.3 cm. x 12.1 cm.)

EIGHTEENTH-CENTURY magazines were natural media for political commentary and pictorial satire, and such works appeared with increasing frequency as Britain's national and international problems mounted. But not all depictions were derogatory or critical in nature. When English military forces were triumphant in battles, or political events at home were stable, then the satiric comment reflected public satisfaction. This frontispiece for the *London Magazine* of 1758 by a little known designer, I. Miller, is an excellent example of this type of print.

Situated in a wooded rocky setting with temple-like buildings in the background, a bearded old man with wings (assumed to represent Father Time) has placed his scythe on the ground in order to use his arms to encircle a globe. It is half turned to show the Atlantic Ocean and North America, locations of present English problems. His gesture suggests that England might be able to control all of the area, part of which still lay under French and Spanish dominion. Father Time glances back over his shoulder toward a figure of a young angel who appears pleased by the present course of events. She holds a banner proclaiming the locations of recent successful English naval engagements: "St. Malo's June 8"; "Louisbourg July 26"; "Cherbourg Augt. 8"; "Frontenac Augt. 27." Standing on a pedestal above is another angelic figure with a laurel wreath. Another maid wearing a similar wreath stands beside Britannia, who holds a staff and shield. The satisfaction evidenced by the figures and the presence of laurel reflect the British victories in the French and Indian War.

B. M. Not listed   1960-134

28

9. *THE ASSES OF GREAT BRITAIN.*

MAKER: J. Jones
PUBLISHER: J. Williams.
DATE: About 1762
SIZE: 12″ x 8″ (30.5 cm. x 20.3 cm.)

THE use of a pictorial design accompanied by a lengthy written commentary, often in verse form, allowed satirists an extra medium to expound on controversial political situations. *The Asses of Great Britain* appeared both in a broadside version with accompanying verses and as a separate engraving. The designer, J. Jones, has skillfully used the age-old definition of ass: a person who is silly or particularly stupid in behavior. In 1762 a number of English leaders, including politicians, writers, and so forth, were engaged in activities that suggested that the word might appropriately be applied to them.

The poem begins as follows:

> Permit me good People (a Whimsical Bard)
> And Snarl not ye Critical Class
> If once I presume without fee or Reward
> To prove that each BRITON'S an ASS.

Among those who fall under this classification are (reading from right to left): the Reverend George Whitefield, an eighteenth-century cleric and evangelist often satirized for his religious fervor and priggish behavior, who sees his image in the mirror as an ass; a Jew placed in stocks;[1] Lord Bute, who rides the bridled English lion and is ac-

cused of making his frightened threats against the people sound like the bray of an ass; the lion, who is accused of being an ass for allowing it to happen; three Cherokee Indians, who have recently arrived from America and are condemned for asinine behavior in admiring and wishing to pay homage to the king; blind magistrate Sir John Fielding, who peers through a telescope and is classified as an ass for continuing to assert that he can tell right from wrong; Henry Howard, the writer famous for composing dull works including a poem "The Queen's Ass";[2] and in the background Charles Churchill, a preacher and one of the most famous satirists of the period, who drives out two more asses, Tobias Smollett, editor of *The Briton*, and Arthur Murphy, associated with *The Auditor,* both progovernment supporters.

B.M. 3941   1960-145

---

1. The position of the Jews in England at this period was very sensitive. Under discussion was the Naturalization Act, which would allow them some amount of freedom but no rights to participate in government. The theme of the Jew and Ass became a popular satiric device to depict the problem; further degradation is suggested by placing the figure in this work in a stock.

2. A zebra had been presented to the queen and was housed in St. James's Park. It was quickly nicknamed "the queen's ass" and Howard produced a poem about it.

J. Jones delin et sculpt.

THE
ASSES of GREAT BRITAIN,
An Answer to
HARRY HOWARD'S ASSES
by FART-inando
A Modern Political Ass-trologer.

Tune the Ass in the Chaplet!

Permit me good People (a Whimsical Bard)
And Snarl not ye Critical Class
If once I presume without fee or Reward
To prove that each BRITON's an Ass.

First view HARRY H———D that Scribling fat Wight
With Forehead well cover'd with Brass
A Dinner is wanting then sits down to Write
And to the whole TOWN shows his A__.

At the best POST in BRITAIN see SAWNEY now Placd
Who thought it wou'd er'e come to Pass
When the LYON should thus be so vilely disgrac'd
And led by the ——— like an ———.

An Ass wee are told found a LYONS rough Hide
And fain for Grim LEO wou'd Pass
But when like the BRITON to frighten he try'd
His Braying discover'd the ASS.

The AUDITOR also attempted to roar
In Billingsgate Wit did surpass
The NORTH BRITON came a good Cudgel he bore
And Smartly Corrected the ASS.

Old SHYLOCK the JEW who in CHANGE ALLEY Strives
The Wealth of the Land to Amass
While into your Pocketts he openly Dives
Of each BULL & BEAR makes an Ass.

Let Sly canting SQUINTUM that sanctify'd Prig
But once take a peep in the Glass
Instead of a Saint with the Spirit grown Big
He'll there see the form of an Ass.

When M——RE sally'd forth the fair Sex to relieve
Like QUIXOTE or Sir HUDIBRASS
That FANNY was Scratching as Truth did believe
But now finds himself a Dull Ass.

Blind JUSTICE who owes the sad loss of his sight
To some unkind Love-inflam'd Lass
May boast he can plainly Discern wrong from Right
JACK CATCH will soon prove him an Ass.

But now to conclude Sirs I think it high Time
This Sing Song Satyrical Farce
And if you dont kindly Encourage his Rhyme
The AUTHOR will look like an Ass.

Publish'd According to Act of Parliament by J. Williams next the Mitre Tavern, Fleet Street London.

THE FISHERMEN.

10. *THE FISHERMEN.*

DATE: About 1762
SIZE: 8″ x 10½″ (20.3 cm. x 26.7 cm.)

THIS print of *The Fishermen* appeared in the same year as the previous satire and continues the discussion of some of the same political problems. Four of the most prominent authors of the day fish in the "Waters of Sedition" outside a country inn. Each airs his own complaint and has brought bags containing "bait" with which he hopes to catch public support of his own particular cause.

To the rear, Arthur Murphy, a contributor to the pro-government publication *The Auditor*, rests against a stack of books that include not only his own works but several legal volumes. He claims that he will be paid for his labor no matter what he does and for bait uses William Pitt's recent pension and affairs surrounding the West Indian trade bill. Wearing native Scotch attire, Tobias Smollett, another loyalist, suggests to Murphy that fishing on the backside of such a pool may not prove too profitable. His bait consists of "Continental Connections" and "Prussian Subsidy," which were subjects of great controversy during the period. A Murphy opponent, Charles Church-ill, with his satiric poem "The Rosciad" protruding from a pocket, swears that he will give up his profession of preaching and devote all of his time to devising means to obstruct and oppose the present government. London lawyer Arthur Beardmore, leaning against a barrel, de-clares that he finds great pleasure in fishing in troubled waters and uses as his bait *The Monitor*, a conservative

paper, "Newfoundland," a colony just lost by the British (but soon to be recaptured), and "Count Bruhl," a strongly disliked minister of state.

The real center of the print, Bute, does not actually appear but is only suggested by the inn, The Scotch House. Born in Scotland, thus making him an intruder in the eyes of most Englishmen, Bute rose rapidly in the ministry. He became the object of hostility and distrust and a natural subject for the political satirist. Word was spread that he intended to enforce censorship on the press. By placing outside his door the fishermen writers, all of varying political views, and with the threat of defection by at least one progovernment supporter, the designer suggests that seditious action may be desirable in order to unseat the powerful Bute.

A verse at the top further describes the situation:

Veluti in Speculo
[Just in observation]

This Scene, as in a Glass presents
The Source of civil Discontents;
Those troubled Waters of Sedition,
Shew, Britons, your distress'd Condition;
And those who fish therein, display
The Kn[ave]s who make your Cash their Prey:

For this they various Baits prepare,
Which only Gudgeons can ensnare:[1]
For Gudgeons catch at e'vry Bait,
And all is Fish that comes to Net.
The Moral of our Allegory,
Sage Politicians! lies before ye.

When ev'ry venal, scribbling Fool,
Presumes to censure those who rule,
Condemn not them:—they write for Bread;
Tis you are most to blame, who read.

Several versions of the print appeared in London at

almost the same time, suggesting not only that the fishermen theme provided a popular vehicle for political comment, but that the political ideologies of the authors depicted were of great public concern.

B.M. 3876   1960-143

---
1. The gudgeon is a small European freshwater fish similar to carp.

11. [A BENJAMIN FRANKLIN SATIRE]

MAKER: Attributed to James Claypoole, Jr.
PLACE: [Philadelphia]
DATE: About 1764
SIZE: 7½" x 9¾" (19.1 cm. x 24.8 cm.)

SURELY no American figure during and through the days of the American Revolution was more the subject of discussion and eventual satire than Benjamin Franklin. His personal and political beliefs coupled with his somewhat rotund physical appearance provided ample inspiration for the caricaturist's pen. Ever involved in international and colonial affairs, Franklin in 1763–64 became deeply concerned about internal conflicts in the Pennsylvania colony. The Paxton Affair had just taken place. A group of Presbyterian Irish from the town of Paxton had murdered a group of Christian Indians in retaliation for attacks by other Indian bands in neighboring areas. In addition the dispute over taxation of wealthy Quaker proprietors and poor landowners had brought the assembly to the point of requesting the removal of the proprietary government.

This satire, published in Pennsylvania probably late in 1764 and believed to have been made by a local artist, James Claypoole, Jr., comments on Franklin's involvement in these matters. A Quaker holding a band of wampum in one hand rides a Scotch-Irish "Hibernian." Around his arm is fastened a leash attached to the nose of a blindfolded German who carries an Indian on his back. Franklin stands to the left holding out a paper that reads: "Resolved / ye Prop[riete]r / a knave / & tyrant / NC D / gov[erno]r D:o."[1] Peeping from between his legs is a small fox, probably representing Joseph Fox, who along with Israel Pemberton was a leader in the Quaker "Friendly Association" and was often accused of supplying money secretly to the Indians. Peering out of a cave, an Indian head observes three dead figures on the ground, implying they had met their death at his hands. In the background a village is in flames.

Beneath the picture is engraved a short verse commenting further on the satire:

> The German bleeds & bears ye Furs
> Of Quaker Lords & Savage Curs
>
> Th' Hibernian frets with new Disaster
> And kicks to fling his broad brim'd Master
>
> But help at hand Resolves to hold down
> Th' Hibernian's Head or tumble all down.

B.M. Not listed   1972-202
                             PROVENANCE: Goodspeed's Bookshop

---
1. In this quotation the abbreviation NC D refers to the Latin phrase *nemine contradicente*, meaning unanimous passage, and was used by Franklin in reference to the assembly's condemnation of the proprietor and governor. For further information on this print see Charles Coleman Sellers, *Benjamin Franklin in Portraiture* (New Haven, Conn., 1962), pp. 379–80.

The German bleeds & bears y.e Furs | Th' Hibernian frets with new Disaster | But help at home Resolves to hold down

Of Quaker Lords & Savage Cur's | And kicks to fling his broad brim'd Master | Th' Hibernian's Head or tumble all down

12. *THE TOMB=STONE.*

MAKER: Attributed to Benjamin Wilson
Printed for Mr. Smith
DATE: [February 1765]
SIZE: 11″ x 17¼″ (27.9 cm. x 43.8 cm.)

CHURCHYARDS, tombs, and vaults have always provided dramatic settings—even for political satirists. Unpopular leaders or annoying laws can be discreetly buried, and tombstones offer a natural stage on which successful politicians may dance in joy while the unsuccessful may prostrate themselves in grief. The 1765 work of Benjamin Wilson, *The Tomb=Stone*, is one of several using this theme to comment on the passage and ultimate repeal of the Stamp Act.[1]

Imposed in March 1765, the act taxed all printed materials in America and was intended to help finance the British troops stationed in the colonies. It was the first direct tax to be levied against them and was bitterly opposed by colonial leaders. The inscription on the tomb explains that William, duke of Cumberland, is buried within. His untimely death is greatly mourned by many who had supported his selection of a ministry opposed to the American stamp act and further excise taxes. Decorating the base of the vault are busts of Britannia and America weeping at his unfortunate fate.

In contrast, dancing jubilantly on top of the tomb encouraged by the Devil and clerics are his foes, pro-taxation political leaders including George Grenville, Lord Bute, Lord Temple, the earl of Sandwich, and the duke of Bedford. A small dog in clerical garb is added to the group. He is labeled *Anti-Sejanus* to represent the Reverend W. Scott, author of a political tract of that title strongly opposing any repeal of the act.[2] From the pockets of each figure protrude papers inscribed with past acts and plans for future levies. The joy of these leaders was short-lived, for they soon found themselves either differing on ideas or completely out of office.

B.M. 4124   1960-35

---

1. For a further discussion of Benjamin Wilson's contributions in the fight against the Stamp Act see M. Dorothy George, *English Political Caricature to 1792* (Oxford, 1959), p. 134.

2. In this and other satires Bute, whose ambition it had been to control English government policy, is often compared to Sejanus, minister to Roman emperor Tiberius, whose plot to overthrow the government led to his capture and death. He had become well known to Englishmen through Ben Jonson's play, *Sejanus,* then still performed in London theaters although it was written in 1603. By the time the Stamp Act was levied Bute had lost most of his actual power in the government, but the public believed that he still controlled many of the leaders.

36

13. *THE REPEAL, OR THE FUNERAL OF MISS AME-STAMP.*

MAKER: [Benjamin Wilson]
DATE: [March 18, 1766]
SIZE: 11½″ x 18″ (29.2 cm. x 45.7 cm.)

ONE of the most famous and popular of the political satires commenting on the Stamp Act is this one, which actually celebrates the demise of the tax. Benjamin Wilson, designer of the previous satire, was responsible for the work. He boasted that it was available for sale within ten minutes of the official repeal.[1] An instant success, it became one of the most copied satires of the period, one version appearing in the *Wochentliche Philadelphische Staatsbote* on May 26, 1766, just two months following the London publication.

A funeral procession composed of supporters of the act carry a small coffin containing the remains of the bill toward an open vault, appropriately adorned with two skulls. It has been prepared for the internment of all unjust acts that would alienate Englishmen. Leading the cortege and preparing to deliver the funeral eulogy is the Reverend W. Scott, who is followed by the mourners: Grenville, carrying the coffin, Bute, Bedford, and Temple, the same government officials whom Wilson had depicted jubilantly celebrating the passage of the act in the previous work.

By setting the action on the dock, Wilson is able to depict the large unshipped cargoes destined for America that accumulated during the period when the act was in force. Ships labeled "Conway," "Rockingham," and "Grafton" that represent Whig leaders responsible for the repeal of the bill now stand ready to carry the goods to their destinations. Stamps just returned from America are also stacked on the wharf. One crate contains the statue of William Pitt, another English leader responsible for the repeal. It is probably the one intended for Charleston, South Carolina, where such a monument was subsequently erected.

Later impressions of the satire carried lengthy explanations of the tax and its repeal beneath the picture.

B.M. 4140   1960-37

---

1. Details on the swift publication can be found in M. Dorothy George, *English Political Caricature to 1792* (Oxford, 1959), p. 135.

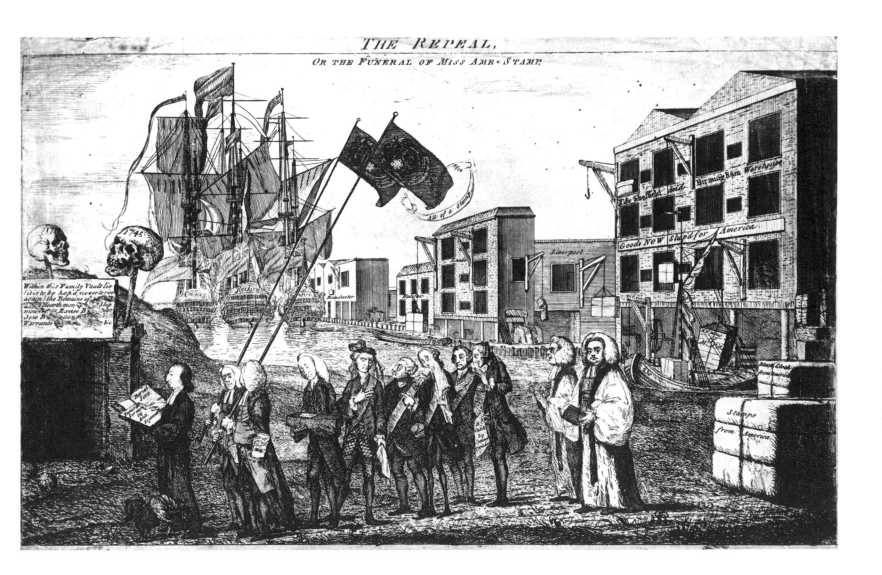

THE REPEAL,
OR THE FUNERAL OF MISS AME=STAMP.

The STATUE, or the ADORATION of the WISE—MEN of the—WEST.

Sold by Mr. Smith No. 45 Long Acre, and Mr. Clagget Junr. in Sugar Loaf Court, Fanchurch Buildings London.
Publish'd April 2t 1766

14. *THE STATUE, OR THE ADORATION OF THE WISE-MEN OF THE-WEST.*

Sold by Mr. Smith and Mr. Clagget, Junior
DATE: April 21, 1766
SIZE: 9¼″ x 11¾″ (22.5 cm. x 29.8 cm.)

THE inspiration of an unknown satirist, *The Statute* continues the commentary on the political leaders responsible for the Stamp Act, and extols the virtures of its repeal. The center of the picture is dominated by a statue of Reverend Scott, which has been paid for by voluntary subscriptions from those who admired his effective eulogy at the burial of the act. On the base of the monument are the names of the donors, some of whom stand admiring the work. Among the gathered notables are Lord Sandwich in the guise of Jemmy Twitcher, George Townshend as Geo. Stamp, and Lord Bute as Sejanus. To the left is the tomb holding the remains of the act, the doors closed signifying the hope that it would remain forever buried. The inscription above describes the demise.

Above the statue hovers the figure of a fury "Repeal." It carries a scourge in one hand and in the other a mirror into which Scott must forever gaze. These, suggest the satirist, are just punishments for his support of the act.

B.M. 4141   1960-38

The Colonies Reduced
Design'd & Engrav'd for the Political Register.

Its Companion.

15. *THE COLONIES REDUCED. ITS COMPANION.*

PUBLISHED: *Political Register.*
DATE: [1768]
SIZE: 8″ x 4¾″ (20.3 cm. x 12 cm.)

DURING the period when the Stamp Act was nominally enforced, English industrial interests were threatened financially by the restrictions placed on colonial trade. Benjamin Franklin, then residing in London as a colonial agent, worked arduously for repeal of the tax, constantly reminding the men in power of the dangers inherent in its continuation. In 1765 he designed a card on which was engraved a picture, *Magna Britannia-Her Colonies Reduced*, which he then had printed early in 1766. Britannia, all her appendages (Virginia, Pennsylvania, New York, and New England) removed, her ships idle in the harbor, is depicted in a destitute position.

There is nothing to indicate that Franklin may have offered the satire for sale in England; rather, he probably distributed it as a propaganda item to influential government and business leaders. However, by 1768 the work had become well known and was copied with only a slight alteration in the title, *The Colonies Reduced*, and it was accompanied on the same sheet by a second satire, *Its Companion*. The two were published in the *Political Register*, a magazine founded in 1767 by John Almon, a London bookseller and writer. England's additional problems are described in the second work. Bute stabs Britannia in the back and thrusts her toward Spain, while at the same time he threatens America, who with only a rattlesnake for protection flees to France for help.[1] While these struggles occur in the foreground, in the rear a Dutchman seizes a boat and runs away with it, a gesture suggesting Holland's determination to dominate trade.

Although the Stamp Act had been repealed by the 1768 date of this work, England's foreign troubles were growing and a satire such as this from Franklin remained timely and well worth the effort needed to reproduce it, particularly for publication in a magazine so dedicated to opposing government policies.

B.M. 4183   1960-39

---

1. In 1754 the *Pennsylvania Gazette* (Philadelphia) printed a political satire believed to have been designed by Benjamin Franklin that portrayed the fragmented colonies as a rattlesnake cut into sections. A snake subsequently became one of the symbols for the colonies.

Avaunt ye troublers of a World's repose,
No more your base destructive schemes disclose:
For GEORGE shall yet support the fainting Fair,
Restore her fleace, & shield her from Despair.

16. *UNTITLED*

PUBLISHED: [*London Magazine*]
DATE: [1768]
SIZE: 7¼″ x 4½″ (18.4 cm. x 11.4 cm.)

IN 1768 the publishers of the *London Magazine* used the frontispiece and preface to comment on the current unsettled state of England's foreign affairs. Pictured is the weeping figure of Liberty, her feet resting on maps of Corsica and North America, both areas where struggles for freedom were taking place. George III and Britannia stand beside her, while a youth representing Corsica kneels before her in a gesture of supplication. In the background the sails of a ship suggest the problems in trade that England was experiencing because of its foreign policies.

Beneath the picture a verse explains:

Avaunt ye troublers of a World's repose
No more your base destructive schemes disclose:
For GEORGE shall yet support the fainting Fair,
Restore her peace, & shield her from Despair.

The preface expressed the hope that George III would act to restore peace rather than destroy it.

B.M. Not listed   1960-135

17. *WORTHY OF LIBERTY, MR. PITT SCORNS TO INVADE THE LIBERTIES OF OTHER PEOPLE.*

MAKER: Charles Willson Peale
DATE: About 1768
SIZE: 23½″ x 15¼″ (59.7 cm. x 38.7 cm.)

NO political leader in England was more vocal in the support of pre-Revolutionary American causes than William Pitt, earl of Chatham, who became the object of much praise and adulation in the colonies. Charles Willson Peale, a colonial artist, was studying in London in 1766 when Pitt appeared before Parliament to plead for the repeal of the Stamp Act. Inspired by the event, Peale twice painted a symbolic portrait of Pitt as a tribute to his zealous efforts. Not content with this, he then engraved the portrait, making it available for sale to all Pitt admirers on both sides of the Atlantic.

Pitt, attired as a Roman consul, stands before an altar with a burning flame, the symbol of the sacred cause of liberty. He holds the Magna Charta in one hand and with the other points toward a statue of British liberty suppressing the petition of the New York Congress for repeal of the Stamp Act. On the pedestal of the statue is the figure of an American Indian watching England's disregard for her colonies' welfare. The altar is adorned with bust heads of Algernon Sidney and Richard Hampden, famous seventeenth-century writers and defenders of liberty.

Whether this work is a true satire may be open to question. Certainly it does not make the derogatory comment most commonly associated with satire. It does, however, present a firm statement on a political situation and portrays the protaganist in a symbolic rather than a realistic guise. Furthermore, when published the print was accompanied by a full explanation of the political situation that inspired the design.

B.M. Not listed

1953-747
PROVENANCE: The Old Print Shop

Worthy of Liberty, M. Pitt scorns to invade the Liberties of other People.

18. *WHAT MAY BE DOING ABROAD. WHAT IS DOING AT HOME.*

PUBLISHED: *Political Register.*
DATE: [1769]
SIZE: 7¼″ x 4⅓″ (18.4 cm. x 11 cm.)

ENGLAND's complex foreign relations and continually worsening internal problems in the late 1760s, resulting from incompetent leadership, provided constant sources of inspiration for the political satirist. Designed for the April 1769 *Political Register*, this two-part work centering on the conference table skillfully depicts the chaotic prospect of England's losing much of its great dominion through ill-conceived policies.

In *What may be doing Abroad* four of the European states previously involved in the 1748 Aix-la-Chapelle conference (see No. 2) now exclude England from deliberations and examine a map in order to divide among themselves the kingdom of Great Britain. Spain, unhappy with a previous settlement, desires Gibraltar, Jamaica, Carolina, and Canada. France wishes Ireland for the young duke of Orleans, Scotland for the young pretender Bonnie Prince Charles, and England for itself. Maria Theresa, ruler of Hungary, Bohemia, and Austria, claims Bengal and Madras in order to establish an East India Company. Finally, the king of Prussia demands all of North America and Hanover.

While this conference is taking place, *At Home* George III is grief-stricken to discover five of his ministers, led by the duke of Grafton, then prime minister, conferring in secret. Their primary concern is not the monumental international crisis that threatens England, but rather a number of small local matters that would further strengthen their own personal political positions and weaken the king's.

B.M. 4287   1960-40

19. *THE EVER-MEMORABLE PEACE-MAKERS SETTLING THEIR ACCOUNTS.*

DATE: About 1769
SIZE: 3¾″ x 6″ (9.5 cm. x 15.2 cm.)

THE Peace of Paris in 1763 ended both the French and Indian War in America and its Continental phase, known as the Seven Years' War. However, many Englishmen, feeling the agreement was unfavorable to Britain, sought explanations from the leaders responsible for it. The satirist depicts three of the leaders involved seated at a table debating the affair.

With the Devil as an accomplice, fox-headed Lord Holland (Henry Fox), sits behind a book labeled "Un-ac[counte]d Millions." The duke of Bedford contemplates four scrolls representing the "West Indies," "North America," "Manillas," and "Neg. 150,000." The earl of Bute, in the middle, places one hand on the tip of a pen

held by Holland in a symbolic gesture of support. During the actual treaty negotiations these leaders were accused of taking bribes in order to assure Spain and France of favorable settlements. British forces that had captured Spanish Manila during the war were promised large sums of money by the Spanish commanders if they would refrain from looting the area. In actuality no such reward was forthcoming, but English leaders still decided to return the city to Spain, thereby causing speculation that they might secretly have received such payment.

B.M. 4300   1960-42

The ever-memorable Peace-Makers settling their Accounts.

20. *THE MACHINE TO GO WITHOUT ASSES.*

PUBLISHED: *Political Register*
DATE: [1769]
SIZE: 4" x 6⅓" (10.2 cm. x 16.1 cm.)

THE *Political Register* of 1769 featured this satire show-ing a self-propelled vehicle aptly named "Magna Charta," its wheels representing "Great Britain," "Ire-land," "America," and "India."[1] Under the guidance of George III, whose steering device is labeled "rights of my people," and Miss Liberty, carrying staff and cap, the machine passes over the crumpled bodies of Grafton, Bute, Holland, and Mansfield. Clinging to the rear for support are three male members of "The Family Com-pact," the kings of France and Spain and an unidentified European nation.[2] The angel "Fame," laurel wreath in hand, hovers above.

The satirist suggests that the king should assume his rightful leadership and dismiss those ministers who wanted to destroy freedom in England and the colonies.

B.M. 4318   1960-43

---

1. A new type of coach had recently appeared, giving Londoners something different to discuss. The vehicle was propelled by a gear manipulated by the driver rather than by horses.

2. The unidentified nation is probably intended to be the Austro-Hungarian empire, although normally in such satires its symbolic representation is female.

The Machine to go without Asses.

21. *PATRIOTICK METEORS*

PUBLISHED: [*London Magazine*]
DATE: [1771]
SIZE: 4¾″ x 7″ (12.1 cm. x 17.8 cm.)

BY 1771 the editors of the *London Magazine* were fully committed to featuring political satires in competition with rival publications such as the *Political Register*. Producing them during the brief lulls in England's otherwise turbulent political life often forced the makers to seek new ways of presenting older or less controversial material. The *Patriotick Meteors* offers an excellent example of such a piece.

Resorting to a very simple and most effective design, the satirist comments on the waning popularity of John Wilkes, Brass Crosby, Wilkes's supporter and the outgoing lord mayor, and bull-headed Frederick Bull, recently elected sheriff. Many domestic issues were involved in the downfall of Wilkes, but the most immediate involved his leadership in the fight to have all parliamentary debates published openly. Shown only as heads, their robes of office heaped on the ground, these leaders are depicted falling like meteors from the heavens into the open jaws of a hippopotamus, "The Gulf of Oblivion." By the date of the print, the turmoil erupting from this dispute was no longer a burning issue, but skillful humor has created the illusion of a momentous occasion.

B.M. 4887   1960-152

PATRIOTICK METEORS

THE GULF OF OBLIVION

Exitus acta probat

22. *THE STATE HACKNEY COACH.*

PUBLISHED: [*London Magazine*]
DATE: [1773]
SIZE: 3¾″ x 6¼″ (9.5 cm. x 15.9 cm.)

IN 1773 England was in very serious trouble as a result of the ill-conceived internal and external policies of its leaders. Political satirists felt an obligation to arouse the public to the dangers that lay ahead for their country. *The State Hackney Coach* designed for the *London Magazine* represents only one of the many prints attempting vainly to accomplish this end.

The maker has resorted to the familiar theme of a coach propelled without horses (see No. 20). Now firmly entrenched as England's political leader, Lord North, controlled by the Devil, has harnessed a group of easily swayed colleagues to the vehicle. However, the satirist has chosen to identify only two of the many possible by a recognizable representation. First in line is Lord Holland (Henry Fox), one of those who rose rapidly in power under North's tutelage. Just under the driver in the last row is a black, a satiric guise for Jeremiah Dyson, lord of the treasury and another of North's coterie.[1] Oblivious to the events about him, George III sleeps peacefully in the coach, a pose often used by satirists to suggest his lack of concern for England's grave problems.

B.M. 5098   1960-154

---

1. *The Padlock*, a play by Isaac Bickerstaff, was currently on the London stage. One of the characters was Mungo, a black, who was easily induced to serve any and all. Dyson, easily swayed by the opinions of others, was quickly awarded this nickname by the satirists.

They go fast whom the Devil drives.

G III

The STATE HACKNEY COACH.

23. *THE WHITEHALL PUMP.*

PUBLISHED: [*Westminster Magazine*]
DATE: [1774]
SIZE: 4″ x 5¾″ (10.2 cm. x 14.6 cm.)

THE Boston Tea Party was an event destined to inspire many English satirists who deplored their country's colonial policies. The *Whitehall Pump* was published in another of the politically oriented periodicals, the *Westminster Magazine*, as its offering of sympathy and support to America and also to compete with the popular *The able Doctor* discussed in the introduction.

By pumping water over her, Lord North attempts to revive Britannia who has fallen over Indian America. Standing behind North a group of supporters encourage his efforts to restore Britannia's vitality. John Wilkes and a companion, strong backers of the colonials, stand on the other side and protest North's aid.

The magazine also printed an explanation of the satire, termed a "Vision," that outlined the ministers' plan to revive Britannia by levying additional taxes and perpetrating other indignities against the colonies in reprisal for the Tea Party. The editor claimed these policies negated all freedoms guaranteed by the Magna Charta, Bill of Rights, and so forth, and declared that should the leaders persist in carrying them out, England would be forced to live in a state of fog instead of grace.

B.M. 5227   1960-46

The Whitehall Pump.

24. *THE MITRED MINUET.*

PUBLISHED: [*London Magazine*]
DATE: [1774]
SIZE: 3 $^{11}/_{16}''$ x 6⅜'' (9.4 cm. x 16.2 cm.)

IN May 1774 the Quebec Act was passed and met with mixed reactions in England, the colonies, and Canada. Although many provisions of the Bill were less controversial than those of the Boston Port Bill and the Massachusetts Act, two of its features were very unpopular. Northern colonists strongly opposed giving areas claimed by Connecticut, Massachusetts, and Virginia to French Canada. Of even greater concern, however, was the granting to the French Canadians of complete freedom to practice Catholicism. At this period no group was more religiously intolerant than the northern colonial Protestants; they were supported by their English counterparts who viewed this section of the act with great alarm.

The unknown satirist has depicted Catholic bishops celebrating the passage of the act by dancing joyfully around it. The Devil encourages Bute, North, and an unidentified minister who were responsible for the bill, while other clerics observe the scene with obvious delight.

B.M. 5228   1960-47

The Mitred Minuet.

J.Dixon invenit et fecit

Published 7 Sep.r 1774.

A POLITICAL LESSON.

25. A POLITICAL LESSON.

MAKER: John Dixon
DATE: September 7, 1774
SIZE: 14¼" x 10" (36.2 cm. x 25.4 cm.)

ON June 1, 1774, the British ordered the port of Boston closed in retaliation for the Boston Tea Party, and stipulated that it remain so until payment had been made for all of the tea destroyed. Simultaneously, Gen. Thomas Gage, royal governor of Massachusetts, ordered the capital moved from Boston to Salem.

This action further inflamed the already angry colonials. News of the continuing rebellion was quickly transmitted back to England, where from the outset public opinion opposed the government's attempts to control the colonies. Satirists were inspired to search for new ideas to portray the events that followed.

Of particular interest are a group of prints which, departing from the more usual hastily etched or engraved style preferred by most satirists, were instead worked in mezzotint.[1] While retaining all of the humor expected of such pieces, they were of greater artistic merit. Rather than the more customary sketchy outlines that merely suggested the person or situation involved, complete figures including well-delineated facial expressions are presented, and backgrounds that normally barely suggested locations are fully developed.

The makers of these curious prints present something of a puzzle for the student of the satire. *A Political Lesson* shown here has been identified as the work of John Dixon,

a little known mid-eighteenth-century engraver. Others are credited to no particular maker, but in the British Museum catalog George suggests that they may have been the work of Philip Dawe, a London engraver known for his social satires of the Macaronies. Since three publishers—John Bowles, Carington Bowles, and Sayer and Bennett—printed them, it is probable that once the idea became successful, it was copied by others. Completely identifiable portraiture was avoided, but the figures and backgrounds are easily recognized.

A Political Lesson was the first to be published. On a lonely country road, a storm brewing overhead, a rearing angry horse has thrown its rider to the ground. Under his head is a portion of a milestone indicating that Boston is six miles away; above, a signpost points to Salem. The rider presumably represents General Gage on his journey to Salem to meet with the reorganized Massachusetts legislature, while the horse symbolizes the rebellious colony throwing off the new challenge to its freedom.

B.M. 5230   1960-128

1. In 1904 R. T. H. Halsey published for the Grolier Club of New York *The Boston Port Bill as Pictured by a Contemporary London Cartoonist*. Primarily concerned with this set of satires, the title has often been used to refer to the group as a whole. For others in the series see Nos. 26, 27, 28, 32, 33, and 34.

A New Method of MACARONY MAKING, as practised at BOSTON.

For the Custom House Officers landing the Tea,   And they drench'd him so well both behind and before,
They Tarr'd him, and Feather'd him, just as you see,   That he begg'd for God's sake they would drench him no more.

Printed for Carington Bowles, at his Map & Print Warehouse, N.º 69 in St Pauls Church Yard, London. Publish'd as the Act directs, Oct.t 12.th 1774.

26. *A NEW METHOD OF MACARONY MAKING, AS PRACTISED AT BOSTON.*

Printed for Carington Bowles
DATE: October 12, 1774
SIZE: 14¼″ x 10¼″ (36.2 cm. x 26 cm.)

ALTHOUGH not directly involved in the Boston Tea Party, John Malcomb was in the unfortunate position of being stationed there as a British customs official. His determination to collect all of the newly imposed duties so angered the Bostonians that on January 24, 1774, they treated him to a typical eighteenth-century punishment, tarring and feathering. Once covered, he was led to the gallows on the edge of town, forced to drink a prodigious quantity of tea, and finally released after being suspended for a time. The two men in charge of administering the punishment wear hats adorned with Sons of Liberty symbols.

When the news of the event reached London it was greeted with hearty approval by colonial sympathizers and inspired this satire that belongs to the set described in No. 25. Carington Bowles first published the work in a small size, but it met with such success that it soon became available in the larger version shown here. A folio edition was printed in 1775.

The verse accompanying the engraving further describes the event:

For the Custom House Officers landing the Tea,
They Tarr'd him, and Feather'd him, just as you see,
And they drench'd him so well both behind and
    before,
That he begg'd for God's sake they would drench
    him no more.

B.M. 5232   1960-127

The BOSTONIAN'S Paying the EXCISE-MAN, or TARRING & FEATHERING

Plate I.

London Printed for Rob.t Sayer & J.Bennett, Map & Printseller, N.o 53, Fleet Street as the Act directs 31 Oct.r 1774.

27. *THE BOSTONIAN'S PAYING THE EXCISE-MAN, OR TARRING & FEATHERING.*

MAKER: Attributed to Philip Dawe
Printed for Robert Sayer & J. Bennett
DATE: October 31, 1774
SIZE: 13¾″ x 10¼″ (34.9 cm. x 26 cm.)

THREE weeks after the appearance of the previous satire (No. 26) the firm of Robert Sayer and John Bennett published its version of the tarring and feathering of John Malcomb. Slightly more complex in design, it has no accompanying verse or explanation. Sayer and Bennett eventually compiled these satires on pre-Revolutionary events into a bound volume; the plate marks on the prints indicate their placement in the work.

The Liberty Tree becomes the gallows in the print, and the tar bucket and dabber can be seen in the lower left corner. Malcomb is depicted spewing out the tea that he is being forced to drink. The background vignette of the Boston Tea Party in progress is an important feature of the satire as it is one of the earliest known pictorial representations of the event. The scene is frequently extracted from the print and is used to illustrate the tea party.

B.M. listed at 5232   1960-126

The BOSTONIANS in DISTRESS.

London, Printed for R. Sayer, & J. Bennett Map & Printsellers, N° 53 Fleet Street, as the Act directs 19 Nov.ᵣ 1774.

28. *THE BOSTONIANS IN DISTRESS.*

MAKER: Ioh[n] Marlin Will
Printed for Robert Sayer, & J. Bennett
DATE: November 19, 1774
SIZE: 14¾″ x 9¼″ (37.5 cm. x 23.5 cm.)

ONLY three weeks after publishing the satire on John Malcomb the Sayer and Bennett firm issued a second work commenting on the Bostonians' plight. Immediately after the tea party the British closed the port of Boston, which greatly concerned the other colonies, most Englishmen, and also friendly European nations. When other colonies attempted to send supplies, the English quickly stationed more troops in the area to enforce the blockade.

Two different impressions of the satire are in the Colonial Williamsburg collection, and a third has been recorded.[1] Sayer and Bennett published both of the Williamsburg copies. One credits its making to John Marlin Will of Augsburg, while the other has no mention of a maker. Will is recorded to have copied a number of the portrait caricatures of both British and colonial Revolutionary leaders, but none of an actual event; it is impossible at the present time to determine whether this was an original Will design.

The maker has symbolized the closing of the port by placing the Bostonians in a cage suspended from the Liberty Tree.[2] Three men in a small boat are attempting to feed the hungry citizens with fish placed on the ends of long poles that are then thrust through the bars. British soldiers on the shore are supported by cannons, and the ships in the harbor symbolize the continued blockade.

B.M. 5241   1960-129

---

1. A mirror image (reversal of positions) of this design is recorded in The Museum of Graphic Art, *American Printmaking, The First 150 Years* (Washington, D. C., 1969), p. 31, no. 43.

2. The use of a cage to represent the closing of a port was not a new satiric device. At No. 4 in this volume Boitard used it to depict the British blockade of the Louisbourg fort during the French and Indian War.

29. *THE COLOSSUS OF THE NORTH: OR THE STRIDING BOREAS.*

PUBLISHED: [*London Magazine*]
DATE: [1774]
SIZE: 6¼″ x 7½″ (15.9 cm. x 19 cm.)

BY the time this print was published in the *London Magazine* the use of a Colossus to depict overwhelming political power had become a well-known satiric device. The designer has adroitly depicted Lord North in such a guise. With his feet firmly placed on two raised blocks labeled "Tyranny" and "Venality," North straddles a stream in which members of Parliament swim. In his left hand North holds a burning torch, America, and in his right schemes to raise funds for the impoverished British exchequer. The reference in the title to Boreas, god of the north wind, further symbolizes the political power that North had acquired in the pre-Revolutionary period.

Wilkes, recently elected lord mayor of London, and Britannia stand on the far side of the stream. Britannia holds a banner protesting that those who should preserve her are actually destroying her. Parliament had attempted to deny Wilkes the seat to which he was elected, and although this move pleased North, it further incensed citizens sympathetic to Wilkes and the colonial cause. As suggested in the subtitle, with his broom Wilkes tries to stem the flow of monsters (members of Parliament) who are easily swept along in the stream of Corruption.

B.M. 5242   1960-50

The Colossus of the North; or The Striding Boreas.

See our Colossus strides with Trophies crown'd,
And Monsters in Corruption's Stream abound.

30. *AMERICA IN FLAMES*.

PUBLISHED: [*Town and Country Magazine*]
DATE: [December 1744]
SIZE: 5¾" x 3⅝" (14.5 cm. x 9.2 cm.)

IN December 1774 the *Town and Country Magazine* published this unusual satire concerning events in the colonies just before the Revolution. Departing from the more customary etched or engraved techniques of the period, the maker used a woodcut; this produced strong contrasts and heavy black areas that lent a heightened drama to the events portrayed.

An old woman, America, is engulfed by flames as her foes add more fuel to the fire. Bute, in highland dress, pumps a bellows labeled "Quebec Bill" representing the act that had given some northern colonial territory to French Canada. Mansfield, abetted by the Devil, fans the flame with "Massachusetts Bay," a reference to the many troubles now harassing that colony. Standing beside America, North holds the Boston Port Bill that had just closed the harbor. A teapot from which liquid is spilling rolls down the steps in front of America to symbolize the Boston Tea Party. Beside and in front of America her friends attempt to extinguish the flames, but to little avail.

B.M. 5282   1960-51

31. *LIBERTY TRIUMPHANT; OR THE DOWNFALL OF OPPRESSION.*

DATE: About 1774
SIZE: 10⅞" x 15" (27.6 cm. x 38.1 cm.)

ALTHOUGH this satire has no publication information or date, the events depicted strongly suggest that it was produced in late 1774 or early 1775. The numbered individuals and groups are identified at the bottom; no further explanation accompanies the print.

The action takes place on a map, with the coast of North America to the right, and England to the left. In the upper left a crestfallen Britannia tells the genius of Britain, a winged figure with a spear, that she is distressed by the conduct of her degenerate sons, the colonies. Just below her are two groups, the one to the right representing the chained ministers led by the all-powerful Lord North, dominated by the Devil. To the left are East India Company merchants who complain that the American

treatment of their goods, particularly the destruction of the tea at Boston and the general refusal of their goods by other colonies, is ruinous to them.

On the other shore Indian Princess America, armed with bow and arrow and supported by her braves, protects the country. Below her a group of Tories lament the loss of their income and political influence as a result of the boycott of English goods. Top right the Goddess of Liberty, holding her pole and liberty cap, and the winged figure of Fame discuss the ardor of Liberty's brave sons, the colonies.

B.M. Not listed   1960-44

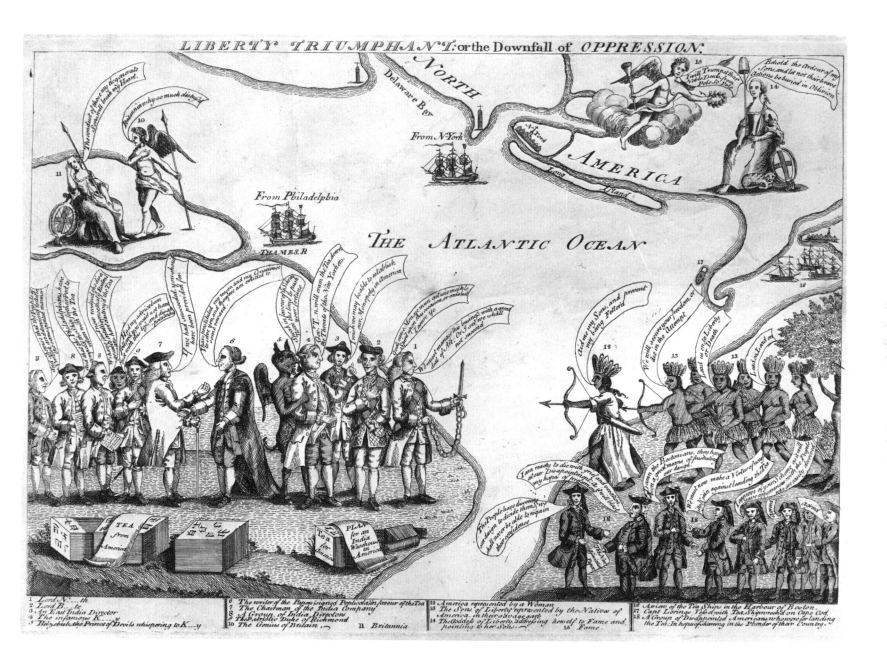

32. *THE PATRIOTICK BARBER OF NEW YORK.*

MAKER: Attributed to Philip Dawe
Printed for Robert Sayer, & I. Bennett
DATE: February 12, 1775
SIZE: 13¾" x 9¾" (34.9 cm. x 24.7 cm.)

THE British extended their blockade of the Boston area to include New York in the fall of 1774, and their troops were garrisoned in the city. In retaliation many New Yorkers refused to cooperate with the soldiers, who were then forced to disguise themselves as civilians in order to obtain essentials. Occasionally their true identity was discovered, resulting in both humorous and serious situations as shown in the incident depicted here. The story was first published on a card in October 1774 and circulated throughout New York. Soon thereafter it became known in England. The London publishing firm of Sayer and Bennett quickly had the tale made into a print to add to their collection of mezzotint satires on the colonial rebellion.

Capt. John Crozer, commander of a British ship, has come unrecognized to the shop of Jacob Vredenburgh, a well-known New York Son of Liberty and barber. A messenger appears in the doorway with a government order for the partially shaved Crozer, thus revealing his true identity. Razor in hand, barber Vredenburgh threatens the captain and sends him running from the shop still lathered. Although the verse has been trimmed from the Colonial Williamsburg impression, it has been retained on others and relates the tale:

> Though Patriot grand, maintain thy Stand,
> And whilst thou sav'st Americ's Land,
> Preserve the Golden Rule:
> Forbid the Captains there to roam,
> Half shave them first, then send 'em home,
> Objects of ridicule.

Through a display of objects in the shop such as wig boxes labeled with the names of important persons, the unknown maker has demonstrated an astute knowledge of the New York liberty movement. On the wall hang prints of Lord Chatham (William Pitt) and Chief Justice Charles Camden, two Englishmen highly esteemed for their support of colonial causes.

B.M. 5284   1960-130

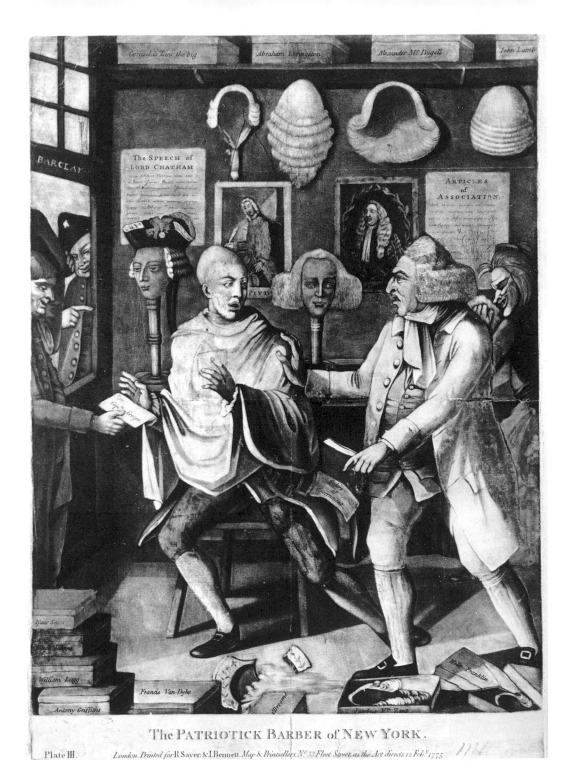

BARCLAY

The SPEECH of
LORD CHATHAM

ARTICLES
of
ASSOCIATION.

PITT

Isaac Sears

William Lugg

Antony Griffiths

Francis Van Dyke

Broome

Jacobus VD Zant

Watt Franklin

The PATRIOTICK BARBER of NEW YORK.

Plate III.   London Printed for R. Sayer & I. Bennett, Map & Printsellers, No. 53 Fleet Street, as the Act directs 12 Febry 1775

33. *THE ALTERNATIVE OF WILLIAMS-BURG.*

MAKER: Attributed to Philip Dawe
Printed for Robert Sayer, & J. Bennett
DATE: February 16, 1775
SIZE: 10⅓″ x 14¼″ (26.2 cm. x 36.2 cm.)

THESE mezzotint satires depicting colonial protests against the Intolerable Acts closely followed the events as they happened.[1] In August 1774 the Williamsburg Resolutions were passed and by February 1775 Sayer and Bennett had published this commentary on the citizens' reactions. Virginians were urged to sign a pledge of loyalty to the resolves of the Continental Congress and to withhold the export of tobacco, the colonies' major and most profitable crop, until all taxes on imported goods were repealed.

In the capitol courtyard at Williamsburg liberty fighters have suspended a plank across two tobacco barrels to serve as a table upon which the pledge has been placed for signing. One of the barrels is labeled tobacco, a gift intended for John Wilkes, lord mayor of London, in appreciation for his support of colonial causes. Some of the colonists appear reluctant to sign the pledge, because curtailing the export of tobacco would cause great financial loss. The alternative is obvious: behind the table, suspended from a gallows, are barrels of tar and feathers.

In the left background is a statue honoring Lord Botetourt, the highly respected royal governor of Virginia from 1768–70, which was erected in 1774 as a symbol for what was then British-American unity. This is the earliest known depiction of the monument, which now stands in the gallery of the Earl Gregg Swem Library at the College of William and Mary, Williamsburg, Virginia.

B.M. Listed in 5284   1960-131

_____

1. The name Intolerable Acts was given to the series of bills passed by Parliament to punish the colonies following the Boston Tea Party.

A CURE FOR THE REFRACTORY

BOTETOURT

TOBACCO.
A PRESENT

For
JOHN WILKES
Esq.

LORD MAYOR OF
LONDON.

LIBERTY

Non Importation

THE ALTERNATIVE OF WILLIAMS·BURG.

Plate IV.

London Printed for R. Sayer & J. Bennett, No. 53 Fleet Street, as the Act directs 16 Feb. 1775.

34. *A SOCIETY OF PATRIOTIC LADIES, AT EDENTON IN NORTH CAROLINA.*

MAKER: Attributed to Philip Dawe
Printed for Robert Sayer, & J. Bennett.
DATE: March 25, 1775
SIZE: 14″ x 10″ (35.6 cm. x 25.4 cm.)

PUBLISHED in March 1775 by Sayer and Bennett, this was the last of the series of mezzotint satires commenting on the pre-Revolutionary plight of the colonies. The unknown designer has changed the location to Edenton, North Carolina, and has shifted the attention from the masculine to the feminine aspects of the controversy.

A group of women have gathered in the parlor of a fashionable home to sign a loyalty oath similar in content to that presented to the Williamsburg citizens in the previous work (No. 33). A woman of stern countenance presides at one end of a table upon which rests the document to be signed. Inscribed on it is the following resolve:

> We the Ladys of Edenton do hereby solemnly Engage not to Conform to that Pernicious Custom of Drinking Tea, or that we the aforesaid Ladys will not promote ye wear of any Manufacture from England untill such time that all Acts which tend to Enslave this our Native Country shall be Repealed.

One lady bends over the table to add her signature while on the other side another is distracted by the attentions of a gentleman who has intruded into the female sanctuary. Directly behind stand two women, one drinking an alternative to tea from a large punch bowl. In the doorway three women pour the contents of tea caddies into the hats of men who will take it away. Other empty caddies suggest the real sacrifice these ladies are making in behalf of the cause. The unknown maker has added a delicate touch to the otherwise stern reminders of the difficult times by placing a small child under the table playing with a miniature tea set. A pet dog affectionately licks the child's face while it urinates on a tea caddy.

B.M. 5284   1960-132

We the Lady's
of Edenton do
hereby Solemnly
Engage not to Conform
to that Pernicious Custom
of Drinking Tea, or that we the
aforesaid Ladys will not promote ye wear
of any Manufacture from England
untill such time that all Acts
which tend to Enslave this our
Native Country shall be Repealed

A SOCIETY of PATRIOTIC LADIES,
AT
EDENTON in NORTH CAROLINA.

Plate V.

London, Printed for R. Sayer, & J. Bennett, Nº 53 in Fleet Street, as the Act directs 25 March 1775.

35. *THE POLITICAL CARTOON, FOR THE YEAR 1775.*

PUBLISHED: [*Westminster Magazine*]
DATE: [1775]
SIZE: 4¼″ x 7″ (10.8 cm. x 17.8 cm.)

IN 1775 the *Westminster Magazine* published this satire which for the first time used the word "cartoon" as part of the title. Unfortunately no explanation accompanied the work, thus leaving the maker's interpretation of the term a mystery. The use of cartoon to denote a humorous piece, whether social or political, did not achieve popular acceptance until the mid-nineteenth century. It is difficult, however, after studying the print to believe that the maker could have expected the viewer to apply to it the accepted definition of a cartoon, that of a preliminary design for a work of art.

The print is a presentation of England's many problems in 1775. Now a common satiric symbol, the coach has two occupants. The driver is Lord Mansfield, an ardent supporter of the ministers in power; the passenger is the king, eyes closed to the chaos around him. Bute, holding papers that refer to his unpopular proposals, "Places," "Pensions," and "Reversions," is the footman. The coach is pulled to the brink of a chasm by horses labeled "Pride and Obstinacy," charges often leveled against the three. The Magna Charta and Constitution are under the wheels of the coach. The Devil flies off with a sack containing the national credit as several bishops and Lord North watch approvingly.

Gathered in the right foreground is a motley group of citizens symbolic of a segment of the rural population easily bribed and corrupted by the ruling English politicians.

B.M. 5288   1960-53

The Political Cartoon, for the Year 1775.

THE CONTRAST.

England   America

Let us not Cut down the Tree to get at the Fruit.

Let us Stroke and not Stab the Cow; For her Milk, and not her Blood, can give us real Nourishment and Strength.

36. *THE CONTRAST*.

DATE: About 1775
SIZE: 10″ x 13⅞″ (25.4 cm. x 35.2 cm.)

BASED on the events depicted, this undated satire may be placed in the period 1775–76. Commenting on England's reconciliation gestures toward the colonies just prior to the outbreak of hostilities, the designer has chosen as his setting a rural landscape, divided by a stream into two sections in which the alternatives of peace and destruction are symbolically portrayed.

Tied to a stump on the left, a cow, representative of America in both scenes, is being stabbed and tormented by a group of men. On the cow's rump is the official stamp of the Stamp Act. A raven perched in a tree is ready to swoop down for the kill. A cloth placed tentlike over the limb of a tree forms a shelter for some of the assailants. To the rear a man chops down a tree laden with apples.

On the right is a contrasting scene of tranquility. The cow, bedecked with floral garlands, is fed by children as a woman milks it; others dance, play, and partake of milk from the animal. Two love birds perch high in an apple tree, while a boy picks the fruit and tosses it to a girl on the ground. Behind, two Indians are on a deer hunt.

The inscription below, couched in biblical terms, continues the designer's appeal for peace:

> Let us not Cut down the Tree to get at the Fruit.
> Let us Stroke and not Stab the Cow; For her milk,
> and not her Blood, can give us real Nourishment
> and Strength.

B.M. 5298   1960-54

CUPID'S TOWER.

Fair tresses Mans imperial race ensnare,
And beauty draws us with a single hair.

Pub. March 1. 1776 by Marly & g. Strand

BUNKERS HILL
or America's Head-Dress

37. *CUPID'S TOWER. BUNKERS HILL OR AMERICA'S HEAD-DRESS.*

PUBLISHED: Matthew Darly
DATE: March 1, 1776
SIZE: 9½″ x 7″ (24.1 cm. x 17.8 cm.)

THE London shop of Matthew Darly became well known in the early 1770s for its engravings of Macaronies, one of the most satirized of English social fads. The term was contrived to describe dress, hair, and life styles affected by those who traveled on the Continent and, upon their return, greatly exaggerated in their own habits that which they had observed and admired. While none of the eccentricities escaped the eye of the humorist, it was the high, overblown, and ornately curled coiffeurs that provided the greatest inspiration.

These two works from Darly and his wife, Mary, who did most of the engraving, were published on the same plate and demonstrate how suitable the hair style was for both social and political commentary. To the left *Cupid's Tower* depicts an enormous hairdo engulfing a pretty young woman. Perched high on top of it is a very small cupid with bow and arrow. Beneath is inscribed:

> Fair tresses Man's imperial race ensnare,
> And beauty draws us with a single hair.

By contrast, far more alarming is the action occurring on the Macaroni headdress to the right, for now the curls and plateaus have become the setting for the battle of Bunker Hill. The top three sections depict British troops who appear to be firing at each other, while just below colonial troops pull cannons toward the battle. Three flags are inserted in the hair in imitation of the more usual feather accessory.

Two months after this satire appeared the Darlys used the same Macaroni hair style to depict the evacuation of Howe's troops from Boston in *Noodle-Island. Or How. Are we Deceived.*[1]

B.M. 5377   1960-56

---

1. Colonial Williamsburg does not presently have an impression of this satire; it is recorded in the British Museum catalog at No. 5335.

News from America, or the Patriots in the Dumps.

38. *NEWS FROM AMERICA, OR THE PATRIOTS IN THE DUMPS.*

PUBLISHED: *London Magazine*
DATE: November 1776
SIZE: 6½″ x 4¼″ (16.5 cm. x 10.8 cm.)

ONCE the Revolutionary War began, attempts were made to transmit news of battles back to England quickly. Often such reports, if not actually wrong, were far from correct, and later more comprehensive accounts could turn a battle won into a battle lost. Satirists, ever eager to be current, often found themselves in the embarrassing position of a wrong interpretation just as their work was published.

News From America, published in the *London Magazine* in November 1776, is an excellent example of such a misconception. In October news reached London that Gen. George Howe's troops had successfully taken Long Island. The printmaker has depicted a gleeful government ministry—North, Mansfield, Bute, and George III—standing on a platform proclaiming the news to the people. Distressed patriots, including colonial supporter Wilkes, mourn the event, while a disheveled woman holding a liberty cap sits weeping. To the rear more warships sail off across the ocean.

In actuality, only a few days after the news of Howe's victory was received in London the story of his defeat arrived, but too late to stop the printing of this satire.

B.M. 5340   1960-55

39. *POOR OLD ENGLAND ENDEAVORING TO RECLAIM HIS WICKED AMERICAN CHILDREN.*

PUBLISHER: Matthew Darly
DATE: September 1, 1777
SIZE: 8″ x 12⅞″ (20.3 cm. x 32.7 cm.)

SATIRISTS, ever seeking new ideas for their works, frequently found inspiration in the personal and physical gestures and habits of humans. The works that resulted were often far less restrained and inhibited than are similar ones today, as can be seen in this satire.

The Darly shop responsible for the amusing Macaroni satires (see No. 37) issued this lightly etched, somewhat crude print on September 1, 1777. England, symbolized by a wizened old man leaning his crutch on the English shield at his feet, throws lines across the ocean in an effort to regain control of America represented by five men on the opposite shore. At the end of each line a hook has been securely anchored in a man's nose and England pulls on the lines in an attempt to reclaim the colonials. The men make obscene gestures toward the old man; one has turned and bared his buttocks. Printed below is the following parody of a Shakespearean line:

> And therefore is England mained & forc'd to go without a Staff. shakespeare.

A similar impression of the Darly work has been recorded. It has an earlier date, April 1, 1777, and certain important differences—the half-nude figure is now fully clothed, although his back is still turned, and "Atlantic Ocean" is inscribed on the water. Such changes leave open to question the actual publication sequence of the two satires. In particular, the altering of the one figure suggests that Darly may have been reproved for the indelicate depiction and was requested to alter it. Thus, despite the earlier date on that impression, it may have been printed after the one pictured here.

B.M. 5397   1960-61

Poor old England endeavoring to reclaim his wicked American Children

= And therefore is England maimed & fred to go with a Staff.   Shakespeare.

40. *THE CLOSET*

MAKERS: The Earl of Bute, designer; Lord George
Germain, executer; The Earl of Mansfield, engraver.
PUBLISHER: I. Williams
DATE: January 28, 1778
SIZE: 9¼" x 14¾" (23.5 cm. x 37.5 cm.)

COMPOSED of many small scenes, *The Closet* is a complex satire on the future of the American Revolution. The scene is set in the upper right box where George III and his ministers are seated around a table discussing the colonial situation. Goaded by the Devil, Bute urges bold and resolute action. George, seated next to him, assures the group that he will be firm. Holding a code of laws for America, Lord Mansfield declares that George must kill the colonies before they kill him. Lord George Germain clutches papers that contain instructions for the British commanders in the colonies.

At the bottom right is a group of four figures that have not previously appeared in the satires in this volume. The man with a gun at his head and the prone figure represent Charles Yorke before and after his death. Under much duress Yorke accepted appointment as Lord Chancellor and died almost immediately thereafter, leading to speculation that he had committed suicide. To Yorke's left is the figure of a fool who declares himself firmly for folly, convinced that the present government's policy is foolery. To Yorke's right a headless figure holds his head in his arm. In his other hand is an address of loyalty to the king from Manchester, one of the first towns to support George's colonial policies. The figure's condition suggests that threats were made to obtain such allegiance.

In the center are ships representing three naval engagements. The top, "Quebec Hoy," symbolizes the problems created by the unpopular Quebec Act. The two American privateers in the middle have cut off British shipping from the colonies. At the bottom a group of wounded men are putting ashore from the "Chelsea Hoy." One of the first Revolutionary War incidents had occurred in May 1775 when a British vessel in the Mystic River at Chelsea, Massachusetts, was captured by colonial militia under generals John Stark and Israel Putnam.

The four boxes at the left depict four prewar incidents. At the top the scalping murder of Jane McCrea by an Indian is shown. Loyalist Jane was on her way to her wedding under Indian escort when one of them turned and killed her. Her death incensed both the English, who were helpless to discipline the Indian without incurring further trouble with his tribe, and the Americans, who used Jane's murder for propaganda purposes.

Additional Indian atrocities are shown in the second box. While not actually ordered by the English, some of the abuses may have been encouraged by them. In 1776 The Cedars, an American post on the St. Lawrence, surrendered to an invading party of Canadian regulars and Mohawks, after they agreed to protect the prisoners. Despite assurances, however, a number of Americans in the fort were brutally killed.

The third box shows Burgoyne's retreat following the battle at Saratoga. Dressed in doublet and cavalier boots instead of a uniform, Burgoyne leads a group of shackled soldiers away from the American troops stationed on the hill.

In the last box wounded Scottish soldiers who had

formed part of Burgoyne's army flee the battle scene in disarray.

The maker of this work has added another satiric touch. By including in the publication line the names of politicians he suggests that they must take full responsibility for its content.

B.M. 5470 1960-60

41. *A PICTURESQUE VIEW OF THE STATE OF THE NATION FOR FEBRUARY 1778.*

PUBLISHED: [*Westminster Magazine*]
DATE: [March 1, 1778]
SIZE: 4″ x 6¾″ (10.2 cm. x 17.1 cm.)

THIS English satire representing the state of the nation early in 1778 was one of the most popular and most copied works of the Revolutionary era. The Colonial Williamsburg collection contains four distinct impressions: that shown here, one in French, and two different versions in Dutch.[1] The *Westminster Magazine* impression separated the explanation from the picture, while the Continental impressions, published as individual prints, placed the description immediately under the design.

The shoreline, so often used in prints of this period, has been selected for the setting. Representing England's commerce, the cow stands passively while an Indian, symbolizing America, saws off its horn. Its other horn has already been removed and is on the ground. Milking the cow, a grinning Dutchman has passed large bowls of the fresh liquid to a Frenchman and a Spaniard who appear satisfied with their share. An Englishman, wringing his hands in despair, stands in front of the cow. Next to him the British lion sleeps oblivious to everything including a dog raising its leg to urinate on the lion's back.

Across the ocean the ship *Eagle* has gone aground just below Philadelphia. Between the city and the shore two men are sprawled in drunken apathy around a table with an empty barrel and bottles nearby. In September 1777 Philadelphia had fallen to the British, but the victory was disappointing because the town had been partially abandoned by the Americans.

B.M. 5472, 5726, 5757 1960-68

---

1. In addition to the various impressions in the Colonial Williamsburg Foundation collection and in the British Museum there exist an American impression, attributed to Paul Revere, which changes the location from Philadelphia to New York, an unrecorded English version in reverse, and a French wash drawing of the subject presently in the Library Company of Philadelphia and discussed in its annual report for 1970, pp. 48–49.

A Picturesque View of the State of the Nation for February 1778.

42. *THE COMMISSIONERS.*

PUBLISHER: Matthew Darly
DATE: April 3, 1778
SIZE: 10″ x 14″ (25.4 cm. x 35.6 cm.)

IN 1778 five men were appointed to attempt to negotiate a peaceful settlement of the disputes with colonial America. They kneel before an Indian Princess America who is encircled by a laurel wreath halo and supports the pole and liberty cap. Her back half turned to the commissioners, she is seated on a pile of containers, some of which hold tobacco bound for several European nations but not for England.

Supplications and entreaties pour from the mouths of the five: Lord Admiral Richard Howe, Gen. Sir William Howe, Lord Frederick Carlisle, William Eden, and Commodore (Governor) George Johnstone. They admit that England has committed wrongs in her dealings with America, beg her forgiveness, and suggest that she submit to their domination, although with certain reservations and concessions.

Although the actual commission had not been officially approved by government leaders, Darly published the satire on April 1, 1778. Both Howes refused to make the journey under Carlisle's leadership; therefore, only three commissioners actually came to America. What might have been a total publishing fiasco for the Darlys was averted when America concluded a treaty of alliance with France, thus truly allowing her to turn her back, as pictured, on the English delegation.

B.M. 5473

1960-63

THE COMMISSIONERS.

43. *THE COMMSIONERS INTERVIEW WITH CONGRESS.*

PUBLISHER: Matthew Darly
DATE: April 1, 1778
SIZE: 8½″ x 12¾″ (21.6 cm. x 32.4 cm.)

PERHAPS to correct the mistake made in the previous work (No. 42), the Darly shop issued a second satire commenting on the three commissioners' visit to the colonies. The English group—Lord Carlisle, Eden, and Governor Johnstone—are pictured in foppish garments with appropriate gestures, alluding to the general opinion that they were not capable of coping with such negotiations. They are accompanied by Lord Bute in his Scottish attire. Although he was out of the government and did not go to America, it was believed that he still controlled much of the policy of the leaders. The three American congressional members are portrayed as peasants with blunt features and dressed in odd fur-trimmed gowns and hats reminiscent of the liberty cap. They appear to be dictating the terms of the settlement.

Darly's inspiration for the design may have derived from a speech delivered by the duke of Richmond following reports that one member of the colonial congress had worn such a woollen cap during a council session. The duke decried the necessity that required British noblemen of European manner and polish to negotiate with such peasants.

B.M. 5474   1960-64

The Commsioners interview with CONGRESS.   Pub'd by MDarly 39 Strand April 1. 1778.

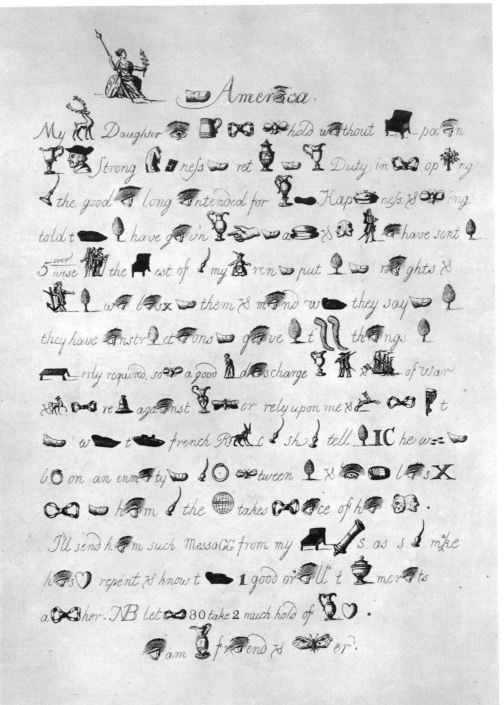

44. *REBUS 1 [BRITTANIA TO AMERICA]*

PUBLISHER: Matthew Darly
DATE: [May 6, 1778]
SIZE: 13¾″ x 9½″ (34.9 cm. x 24.1 cm.)

THE rebus is one of the oldest forms of satiric design. Small appropriate pictures replace letters in words, forming a puzzle that thus challenges the viewer to discover the true meaning of the work. The Darlys used the device in 1778 to write two political letters. In the first Britain pleads with America to put aside the recently formed French alliance and return to her dominion. If the symbols of the letter are interpreted properly it reads as follows:

(Britannia) (toe) Amer(eye)ca.[1]

My (deer) Daughter (eye) (can)(knot) (bee)hold w(eye)thout (grate) pa(eye)n (ewer) (head)strong (back)-(ward)ness (toe) ret(urn) (toe) (ewer) Duty in (knot) op(posy)ng (awl) the good (eye) long (eye)ntended for (ewer) (sole) Hap(pie)ness & (bee)ing told t(hat) (yew) have g(eye)v'n (ewer) (hand) (toe) a (base) & (double-faced) (Frenchman) (Eye) have sent (yew) 5 $\frac{over}{wise}$ (men) the (grate)est of (awl) my (child)ren (toe) put (yew) (toe) r(eye)ghts & (hope) (yew) w(eye)[11] l(eye)s-(ten) (toe) them & m(eye)nd w(hat) they say (toe) (yew) they have (eye)nstr(yew)ct(eye)ons [instructions] (toe) g(eye)ve (yew) t(hose) th(eye)ngs (yew) (form)erly

required. so (bee) a good (girl) d(eye)scharge (ewer) (soldiers) & (ships) of war & (doe) (knot) re(bell) aga(eye)nst (ewer) (moth)er rely upon me & (doe)(knot) (console)t [consort] to w(hat) t(hat) french R(ass)c(awl) sh(awl) tell (yew) IC he w(ants) (toe) b(ring) on an enm(eye)ty (toe) (awl) (union)[2] (bee)tween (yew)& (eye) (but) l(eye)s(ten) (knot) (toe) h(eye)m (awl) the (world) takes (knot)(eye)ce [notice] of h(eye)[s] (doubleface). I'll send h(eye)m such MessaGG [messages] from my (grate) (gun)s as s[h](awl) make h(eye)s (heart) repent & know t(hat) (one) good or (eye)ll t(urn)mer(eye)ts a (knot)her. NB let (knot) (eighty) [hate][3] take (two) much hold of (ewer) (heart).

(Eye) am (ewer) fr(eye)end & (moth)er.

B.M. listed following 5474   1960-65

---

1. Mary Dorothy George transcribed a large portion of the rebus in the British Museum catalog. Toe should be read as "to" throughout; eye substitutes for an "i."

2. Pictured in the rebus is a snake, which was the common symbol for colonial union at the time.

3. To use eighty as a rebus device for hate is a rather obscure reference depending on the pronounciation of hate without an "h."

Published 12th May, 1794 by LAURIE & WHITTLE, No. 53, Fleet Street, London

45. REBUS 2 [AMERICA TO HER MISTAKEN MOTHER]

PUBLISHER: Laurie & Whittle[1]
DATE: [May 12, 1794]
SIZE: 13¾″ x 9¾″ (34.9 cm. x 24.7 cm.)

THE Darlys followed the rebus letter from Britannia to America with America's reply. The Indian princess, now the most frequently used symbol for America, holds in one hand the newly designed thirteen-stripe flag and in the other a fleur-de-lys representing the recently formed alliance with France. The letter reads:

(America) (toe) her (miss)taken (moth)er.

(Yew) s(eye)lly (old woman) t(hat) (yew) have sent a (lure) (toe) us is very (plain) (toe) draw our at(ten)t(eye)on [attention] from our re(awl) (eye)ntrests (butt) we are determ(eye)n'd (toe) ab(eye)de by our own ways of th(eye)nk(eye)ng (Ewer) (five) (child)ren (yew) have sent (toe) us sh(awl) (bee) treated as V(eye)s(eye)tors, & safely sent home aga(eye)n[2] (Yew) may (console)t them & adm(eye)re them, (butt) (yew) must (knot) (x)pect (one) of (ewer) (puppet)s w(eye)ll (comb) home (toe) (yew) as sweet as (yew) sent h(eye)m, twas cruel (toe) send so pretty a (man) so many 1000 miles & (toe) have the fat(eye)gue of re(urn)ing (back) after (spike)(eye)ng h(eye)s (coat) & d(eye)rt(eye)ng [dirtying] t(hose) red (heel) (shoes) [shoeheels] (Eye)f (yew) are w(eye)(eye) [wise] follow (ewer) own ad(vice) (yew) gave (toe) me take home (ewer) (ships) sold(eye)(ears) guard (well) (ewer) own tr(eye)fl(eye)(ling)[3] [trifling] & leave me (toe) my self as (eye)am at age (toe) know my own (eye)ntrests. W(eye)thout (ewer) (fool)(eye)sh ad(vice) & know t(hat) (eye) sh(awl) (awl)ways regard (yew) & my Brothers as relat(eye)ons (butt) (knot) as fr(eye)ends.

(Eye) am (yewer) (grate)ly (eye)njured
Daughter Amer(eye)k.

B.M. 5475   1960-66

---

1. The Darly imprint has been removed not only from this impression but also from that in the recorded British Museum copy. The Laurie & Whittle publication line with a much later date has replaced it. An impression in a private collection records the early Darly printing.

2. A reference to the commissioners sent to America to negotiate a peaceful settlement of the conflict. (See Nos. 42 and 43.)

3. Ling is a fish of the cod family found in North Atlantic waters.

A VIEW IN AMERICA IN 1778

46. *A VIEW IN AMERICA IN 1778*

MAKER: M. Darly
PUBLISHER: Matthew Darly
DATE: August 1, 1778
SIZE: 8⅞″ x12½″ (22.5 cm. x 31.8 cm.)

THIS satire was published just one month after the last important northern battle of the Revolution, fought at Monmouth, New Jersey, June 28, 1778.[1] It comments on the state of affairs in the Continental army at that point in the war, and it is one of the few instances where the maker used America exclusively for the setting.[2] This is one of the most difficult works to interpret, for it is rare that a colonial black appears so conspicuously. The following is only one possible explanation.[3]

At the center, attired in an elegant uniform, an expression of satisfaction on his face, stands Sir Henry Clinton, British commander in chief. With his tricorn hat he directs attention to a black lying on the ground, his wound obvious to all. Clinton faces a man wearing a long fur-trimmed coat and smoking a pipe who probably is intended to represent Baron von Steuben, a former Prussian officer hired late in 1777 to assist in training and commanding colonial troops.[4] Steuben appears unconcerned about the fate of the black as he points to a face buried in his cuff that may represent Charles Lee, a former British officer, now second in command to Washington and considered a hero by the colonials until the battle of Monmouth.

Expecting a major attack in the area, Washington stationed Steuben near Monmouth to watch Clinton's movements carefully, while Lee was charged with the defense. Shortly after fighting began Lee, for reasons that are still not completely understood, misjudged the progress of the battle and, believing it lost, ordered a general retreat. On hearing the news, Washington was incensed and sent Steuben to assume command. Lee was arrested and later was court-martialed. Steuben successfully rallied the troops but, although they bombarded the English forces throughout a long hot day, the Americans were unable to win a clear-cut victory. Clinton, pessimistic about his army's position, decided to retreat quietly under cover of night.

The satire focuses on a problem that was of particular concern to the colonists, that of the blacks who were known to be fighting on both sides during this and other battles in the area.[5] Clinton's position suggests that the black was under his command and that Steuben's American forces were responsible for wounding him. A group behind represents the ambivalent feelings of the colonists. Yankee Doodle Dandy America (identified by the feather in his cap) smiles his approval at the wounding of an enemy as he acknowledges those responsible, a group of ragged colonial soldiers. The soldiers, however, appear distressed because they have wounded one who should have been on their side. Steuben's gesture toward the concealed face in his cuff suggests that he believes the black's disloyalty to his new homeland to be as serious a mistake as Lee's withdrawal.

In the background a lone soldier in the American fort continues to cannonade the enemy.

B.M. 5482   1960-67

---

1. Matthew Darly, publisher of this satire, was well known for the speed with which he could produce a work after an important event had occurred. (See the commissioner satires at Nos. 42 and 43.)

2. See the series based on the Intolerable Acts shown at Nos. 25, 26, 27, 28, 32,

33, and 34 for a major group of satires with American settings.

3. The entry for this work in the British Museum catalog is vague and leaves the question of interpretation open.

4. Steuben's fine clothes were far superior to the uniforms of the colonial forces. His habit of wearing them everywhere caused considerable comment and much ridicule.

5. For a full discussion of the role of blacks in the Revolution see Benjamin Quarles, *The Negro in the American Revolution* (Chapel Hill, N. C., 1961).

47. *THE TEA-TAX-TEMPEST, OR THE ANGLO-AMERICAN REVOLUTION.*

MAKER: Attributed to Carl Guttenberg of Nuremburg
PLACE OF PUBLICATION: [Paris]
DATE: [1778]
SIZE: 16″ x 19½″ (40.6 cm. x 49.5 cm.)

FRANCE formally allied itself to the Revolutionary struggle in 1778. This move forced other Continental nations to reassess their positions toward both England and America. Dutch and French satirists rapidly increased publication of appropriate pictorial comments, which were generally similar in procolonial sentiment to those of their English counterparts. In 1778 Carl Guttenberg, a Nuremberger working in Paris, published this controversial satire based on *The Oracle*, which had been designed and issued in England by John Dixon in 1774.[1]

With his magic lantern Father Time depicts previous events and predicts future expectations. Four dismayed females, symbolic of the four corners of the world, watch his prophecies. A French cock, pumping a bellows, fans an already hot fire over which a teapot has reached the boiling point, spewing its contents—a serpent and a liberty cap—into the air. A small British lion lies under the fire, while to the left three animals presumably representing Spain, Portugal, and Holland fight among themselves. Behind them a group of British soldiers are in retreat, while on the right colonial soldiers led by Indian Princess America advance toward the flames to rescue the liberty cap before it falls into the fire.

Colonial Williamsburg owns two impressions of this work. One is a proof before lettering was added at the bottom; the other is the complete one shown here. Two circular medallions portray historic events that closely paralleled the colonists' fight for freedom. On the left is an auto-da-fe (burning at the stake) commemorating the 1560 religious uprising in Holland. On the right, Wilhelm Tell, a Swiss citizen actively engaged in the struggle for individual freedom in 1296, is shown shooting an apple from the head of his son with a bow and arrow.

For political reasons Guttenberg was forced to remove the French cock from later impressions of the satire. In another version that appeared in England in 1783 the cock was restored, suggesting that France should be held responsible for the Revolution.

B.M. 5490   1960-125

---

1. Colonial Williamsburg has neither *The Oracle* nor the 1783 *Tea Tax Tempest* in the collection, but full descriptions may be found in the British Museum catalog, Nos. 5225 and 6190.

The Tea-Tax-Tempest, or the Anglo-American Revolution.

Ungewitter entstanden durch die Auflage auf den Thee in America.

Orage causé par l'Impôt sur le Thé en Amerique.

48. DEDIÉ AUX MILORDS DE L'AMIRAUTÉ ANGLAISE PAR UN MEMBRE DU CONGRÉS AMÉRICAIN
(Dedicated to the Lords of the English Admiralty by a member of the American Congress)

PLACE OF PUBLICATION: Boston, published for Corbut; Philadelphia, published for Va de bon coeur.
DATE: 1778
SIZE: 6⅝" x 10¼" (16.8 cm. x 26 cm.)

TWO unusual satires with similar publication information suggesting that they were of French origin appeared in 1778 (see No. 49). Although advertised as being drawn in Boston by Corbut and engraved in Philadelphia by "Va de bon coeur" there is no other evidence that they were made in America.

The satire comments on European aid to the colonists as the Revolutionary struggle continued. Explanations of the numbered figures appear below with a brief humorous verse. England, symbolically pictured as half-man, half-vulture, is tied to a tree. Representing America, an Indian trims its claws, a Spaniard holds one wing so that a Frenchman can clip it, and a Dutchman plucks feathers, representing trade, from the other wing while a companion packs them and carries them away. To the left rear another Frenchman is holding rolls of tobacco, while a despairing Englishman standing in the doorway is breaking pipes for which he no longer has use. An unidentified town is shown in the distant right. No inhabitants are visible suggesting that the satirist intends it to represent Philadelphia, which had been abandoned by its population just prior to the date of the print.

The verse below reads:

> Tel qu'un âpre Vautour dévorant l'Amérique,
> Anglais, impunément tu crûs la mettre a sac:
> Mais pour la bien venger d un traitement inique
> Il ne t'y reste pas une once de Tabac.

It suggests that the greedy English vulture devouring America by unjust treatment should be deprived of its much loved tobacco.

B.M. listed following 5472   1960-69

Dessiné d'après nature a Boston par Corbut en 1778 , et gravé à Philadelphie par Va de bon cœur

DEDIE AUX MILORDS DE L'AMIRAUTÉ ANGLAISE PAR UN MEMBRE DU CONGRÉS AMÉRICAIN

1. Un Amiral attaché a un arbre, ayant aux pieds et aux mains des serres de Vautour et des ailes. 2 Le Congrès Américain lui coupe celles des pieds. 3 l'Espagnol tient une des ailes tandis qu'un Français 4 la lui coupe pour empecher son vol. 5 Un autre Français emporte des rouleaux de Tabac. 6 Un Anglais au désespoir casse ses pipes. 7 Un gros Hollandais s'enrichit des plumes qu'il arrache de l'autre aile du Vautour, tandis que son associé 8 fait le commerce à la barbe de l'Angleterre.

Tel qu'un âpre Vautour dévorant l'Amérique,
Anglais, impunément tu crûs la mettre a sac:

Mais pour la bien venger d'un traitement inique
Il ne t'y reste pas une once de Tabac.

49. *DÉDIÉ AUX GÉNÉRAUX DE L'ARMÉE DE LA GRANDE BRETAGNE PAR UN ZELATEUR DE LA LIBERTÉ*
(Dedicated to the Generals of the army of Great Britain by a zealot of liberty)

PLACE OF PUBLICATION: Boston, published by Corbut; Philadelphia, published for Sans souci.
DATE: 1778
SIZE: 6¾" x 10¼" (17.1 cm. x 26 cm.)

A SECOND satire comments on the recent Franco-American alliance (see No. 48). The numbered figures are explained at the bottom, and there is a short humorous poem.

France appears in the guise of an avenging angel carrying a sword and a shield adorned with Medusa's head as she attacks fleeing British troops. One soldier raises his hand in terror, while others fall to the ground in fear, their flag torn to shreds by the angel. To the right a group of colonial citizens celebrate the French alliance by dancing around a maypole that now has the liberty cap added at the top. The American flag has been placed within the circle. In the background Philadelphia appears deserted. Before the British occupied the city significant colonial activities had been removed and much of the populace had fled. On June 18, 1778, Americans reoccupied the city and the British were forced to flee. A white flag of surrender appears on the wall of the city.

The verse beneath reads:

> Anglais audacieux, L'Ange Exterminateur
> Sauve Philadelphie de votre affreuse engeance:
> Contre la trahison, la cruauté, l'horreur,
> Il vient du juste ciel exercer la vengeance:
> Vertueux Insurgens, voyez renaître encor
> Avec la liberté, les jours de l'Age d'Or.

The maker suggests that the avenging angel will come to save the Philadelphians from the cruel and treacherous British and restore the city to a golden age.

B.M. Not listed

1960-59

110

Dessiné d'après nature, a Boston par Corbut en 1778.

Gravé à Philadelphie par Sans souci.

DÉDIÉ AUX GÉNÉRAUX DE L'ARMÉE DE LA GRANDE-BRETAGNE PAR UN ZÉLATEUR DE LA LIBERTÉ

1, L'Ange de la France caractérisé par un bouclier chargé de 3 fleurs de Lys avec une tete de Méduse symbole de la terreur de ses armes. Il tient une epée flamboyante avec
laquelle il chasse les Anglais 2 de Philadelphie. 3 Les Americains se rejouissent de voir renaître l'Age d'Or en Amérique, désigné par le Bonnet de la Liberté 4 avec leur enseigne
attachée à un mât.

Anglais audacieux, L'Ange Exterminateur   Il vient du juste ciel exercer la vengeance:
Sauve Philadelphie de votre affreuse engeance;   Vertueux Insurgens, voyez renaître encor
Contre la trahison, la cruauté, l'horreur,   Avec la liberté, les jours de l'Age d'Or.

50. THE ASSOCIATORS; OR A TOUCH ON THE TIMES.

DATE: About 1778
SIZE: 6⅞" x 10½" (17.5 cm. x 26.7 cm.)

THE unknown maker uses two scenes to comment on the continued inability of the British government to deal satisfactorily with the colonial situation. The box at the left is subtitled "Here Britons view the Man that would have sav'd his Country." The date is 1770, and the man is George III, seated on his throne, who has allowed William Beckford, then lord mayor of London, and a group of his worried supporters to have an audience. A colonial sympathizer, Beckford has come to plead America's cause. Those attending George seem vaguely amused, while his dog yaps at Beckford and his followers.

The second scene is subtitled "There see the Idol who is the instrument of it's ruin." The time is 1778. Lord North, wearing ribbons symbolizing his political ideas, occupies a lofty perch. He is surrounded by all of his loyal supporters. However, a dissenter kneeling close to the steps observes that "they're aw a parcel o loons thus to boo to the Noorth, but ise hold my tongue." The Devil hovers over the group saying, "These are my darling sons, receive them to favor."

Unobserved by the group, the steps to the platform are inscribed with statements concerning the true British situation. They read: "The English Oak is crush'd by the American Reed. May such be the fate of all power founded like the above upon the basis of Corruption L. 10,000 for Col. Reed G. Johnstone, Comr." During the 1778 visit of the English commissioners to the colonies, Johnstone had attempted to bribe Col. Joseph Reed, a member of the American congressional committee. Reed revealed the offer, and Johnstone, already in disfavor for other misconduct, was asked to resign his position when he returned to England.

B.M. Not listed   1960-138

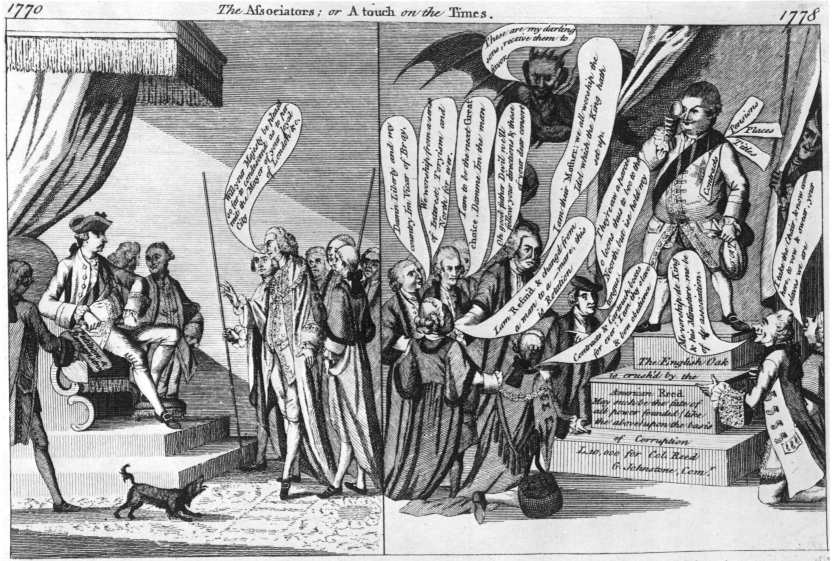

The POLITICAL RAREE-SHOW: or a Picture of PARTIES and POLITICS, during and at the close of the Last Session of Parliament. June 1779.

Published 2.d of July 1779. by Fielding & Walker, Pater-Noster-Row.

51. *THE POLITICAL RAREE-SHOW: OR A PICTURE OF PARTIES AND POLITICS*

PUBLISHER: Fielding & Walker
PUBLISHED: *Westminster Magazine* for June 1779
DATE: July 1, 1779
SIZE: 9½" x 13½" (24.1 cm. x 34.3 cm.)

TWELVE scenes of the many problems confronting the British government in 1779 are the subject of a peep show designed by an unknown satirist for the June 1779 *Westminster Magazine*, published in London on July 1 of the same year. As the operator explains what may be seen, a small boy peers through the hole in the box to view the pictures. Although each segment has a descriptive title, a detailed explanation of the whole was included in the magazine. Comments are as follows, reading from left to right, top to bottom.

1. "The Distressed Financier." Lord North is confronted by creditors who remind him of the financial plight of the government caused in part by the war. The Spanish manifesto refers to Spain's decision to ally itself with France and the colonies.

2. "The Generals in America doing nothing, or worse than nothing." While an unnamed English soldier sleeps in a pose suggesting inebriation, English troops at Saratoga surrender to the Americans, an infamous defeat to most British.

3. "Proving that they have done every thing." Lord North sleeps during a session of the House of Commons as a number of questions concerning government policy are raised. Among the subjects discussed are the course of the war and the court-martial of Sir Hugh Palliser, a member of Parliament who had resigned over the Keppel affair and in turn had been tried. Palliser had insisted that although acquitted, Admiral Keppel be called to account for the defeat of his squadron by the French during the skirmish at Ushant just off the coast of Brittany.

4. "Jemmy Twitcher Overseer of the Poor of Greenwich." Domestic problems were also the cause of much concern. The administration of the royal hospital at Greenwich under the direction of Lord Sandwich, here in the guise of Jemmy Twitcher, was accused of mismanagement and cruelty to pensioners. The popular lieutenant-governor of the complex, Thomas Baillie, was dismissed rather than rewarded for exposing the scandal, and the print shows the seamen pleading with Twitcher for his reinstatement.

5. "The Duke of Richmond turned Linen-Draper." A continuation of the Greenwich hospital case depicts the duke of Richmond appearing in Parliament to defend Baillie's allegations of administrative mismanagement. One complaint was that cloth intended for pensioners' clothing was being diverted to more profitable use by the administrators. Here not only a shirt but also a large piece of material are measured to ascertain if the yardage is correct.

6. "The opposition Pudding-makers." A pudding in opposition to government policy is being prepared. Burke, a strong colonial supporter, carries a basket of flowers, symbols of his wish for peace, while Rockingham, Shelburne, and other sympathizers assemble ingredients for the dish.

7. "Cha. Ja. Tod abusing the national Gamblers." Four men, the most prominent of whom is Fox, here referred

to as Tod, sit around a gaming table. Having been instrumental in the removal of Admiral Palliser and Lord Sandwich from their respective positions in the navy and admiralty, Fox is depicted ready to gamble on attempting to unseat the unpopular Lord North from the government.

8. "The Jerseymen treating the French with Gunpowder Tea." A French expedition attempted to take the small island of Jersey, but the militia drove them off. These small skirmishes were another problem plaguing England in the period.

9. "The Scotch Presbyterians pulling down the Papists Houses." Attacking a Catholic home, a mob destroys religious objects. In February 1779 the No-Popery riots occured in Scotland to express disapproval of the Roman Catholic Relief Act of May 1778.

10. "The English Papists laughing at the Protestants." Four priests and two monks confer about their plans for Catholic domination of England following passage of the Relief Act.

11. "A Picture of Irish Resolution." Another problem concerned Britain's relationship with Ireland, here symbolized by Hibernia, a fainting woman. Ireland adopted a nonimportation act in 1779 to cut off trade with Britain.

12. "Inside View of the Long Room at the Custom House." Starving clerks are shown in an almost empty customhouse, which is the result of the multitude of problems depicted in the other eleven boxes. One clerk sums up the situation very well, "A good Stomach with nothing to eat is very bad."

B.M. 5548   1960-71

52. *THE EUROPEAN DILIGENCE.*

PUBLISHER: William Humphrey[1]
DATE: [October 5, 1779]
SIZE: 7″ x 9½″ (17.8 cm. x 24.1 cm.)

THIS satire by an unknown maker was issued late in 1779 by William Humphrey, a prolific publisher of antigovernment works. A Dutchman is depicted pushing a wheelbarrow occupied by representatives of nations opposing British policies over a prostrate Britannia.[2] A Frenchman stabs at her, encouraged by Indian Princess America, and a Spaniard urges a silent Portuguese to join the alliance. Britannia protests the aid given the colonies by these countries. A reference to the Dutch Island of St. Eustatius, a trade center used to supply arms to the colonies, is on the side of the wheelbarrow.

Another European country is being drawn into the conflict. Russia, depicted as a large burly soldier with musket outstretched, is shown defending England, a situation devoutly desired by the government. Shortly after this work was published, however, Russia issued a declaration of neutrality.

B.M. 5557   1960-72

---

1. The British Museum impression of this satire is dated but lists no publisher; the Colonial Williamsburg impression gives the publisher but no date.

2. The maker has portrayed the diligence (an eighteenth-century term for an open, public carriage) referred to in the title as a wheelbarrow.

THE EUROPEAN DILIGENCE.

53. *THE PRESENT STATE OF GREAT BRITAIN.*

MAKER: J. Phillips
PUBLISHER: William Humphrey
DATE: About 1779
SIZE: 9⅞″ x 15¼″ (25.1 cm. x 38.7 cm.)

THE events depicted in this publication from Humphrey's shop indicate that it was printed at about the same time—1779—as the previous work. Although signed J. Phillips, it is probable that this was a pseudonym then being used by James Gillray. One of the most famous of the late eighteenth-century satirists, Gillray was instrumental in developing the John Bull figure as a new and more modern representation of Great Britain. It has been fairly well established that he was designing works for Humphrey about 1779.[1]

Standing half-asleep, John Bull holds a pole with a liberty cap that the Indian Princess America is stealing. A Dutchman is robbing John Bull of his purse, symbolic of the trade Holland had gained while England was embroiled in wars. A Frenchman rushes toward Bull from the other side but is halted by a figure in Scottish attire. England was actively recruiting troops in Scotland at the time. However, the Scottish were reluctant to participate in the war, and are seldom pictured defending England.

B.M. 5579   1960-73

---

1. Draper Hill, *Mr. Gilray The Caricaturist* (Greenwich, Conn., 1965), pp. 18–19.

Pub.d by W.Humphrey. N.227 Strand.

THE PRESENT STATE OF GREAT BRITAIN.

J.Phillips fecit

54. *JOHN BULL TRIUMPHANT.*

MAKER: Attributed to James Gillray
PUBLISHER: William Humphrey
DATE: January 4, 1780
SIZE: 8⅞" x 13⅜" (22.5 cm. x 34 cm.)

SYMBOLIC of the growing dissatisfaction of the population over events that were bringing the British Empire to the brink of ruin, a large number of antigovernment satires emerged from the print shops during 1780. Occasionally, however, an English victory raised morale and the makers and publishers of satires rushed a progovernment work into print. The Humphrey shop, normally publishers of particularly vicious prints vilifying the government and its leaders, was not insensitive to such changes in feelings, and *John Bull Triumphant* is an excellent example of one of its rare pro-British satires.

The work, believed to have been designed by James Gillray, celebrates the October 1779 victory of the English forces over the Spanish at Omoa in the Bay of Honduras. Large quantities of gold and other cargoes were captured during the battle. The maker symbolizes England as a charging bull that throws Spain high in the air, causing coins to fall out of his pocket. The bull prepares next to attack a frightened Frenchman behind whom Indian Princess America attempts to hide. A Scotsman, representing Bute, pulls on the bull's tail. He is aided by Lord North and Lord Mansfield, a rare instance when these three are depicted in any way restraining rather than attacking the Franco-American alliance. Hiding behind a bush, a Dutchman watches to see how the new turn of events will progress.

Below is a verse of explanation:

> The Bull see enrag'd, has the Spaniard engag'd,
> And gave him a Terrible Toss,
> As he mounts up on high, the Dollars see fly,
> To make the bold Britton rejoice,
> The Yankee & Monsieur, at this look quite queer,
> For they see that his Strength will prevail,
> If they'd give him his way, and not with foul play,
> Still tug the poor Beast by the Tail.

It suggests that the three leaders fear that the English bull could become too strong without their direction, and thus they might lose their powerful government positions. Therefore, it is to their advantage to restrain the beast at this time.

Published on January 4, 1780, the joy of victory would be short-lived, for news had obviously not yet reached London that on December 28 the small garrison left to protect the Omoa fort, ravaged by disease, had surrendered it to the Spanish.

B.M. 5624   1960-74

The Bull see enrag'd, has the Spaniard engag'd,
And gave him a Terrible Toss.
As he mounts up on high, the Dollars see fly,
To make the bold Britton rejoice,

JOHN BULL TRIUMPHANT.

Publish'd Jan.ᵗ 4ᵗʰ 1780. by W. Humphrey Nᵒ 227 Strand.

The Yankee & Monsieur, at this look quite queer,
For they see that his Strength will prevail,
If they'd give him his way, and not with foul play,
Still tug the poor Beast by the Tail.

55. *THE BULL ROASTED: OR THE POLITICAL COOKS SERVING THEIR CUSTOMERS.*

PUBLISHER: John Harris
DATE: February 12, 1780
SIZE: 9¼″ x 13¼″ (23.5 cm. x 33.6 cm.)

IN 1780 John Harris, a lesser known publisher of political satires, provided formidable competition for the more famous shops of Humphrey and Darly. This and the following are samples of works, usually by unidentifiable artists, issued by him.

The bull, now symbolic of England, is being roasted on a spit, tended by the leaders who must share responsibility for its demise. Turning the spit, George III complains that it has made him sweat. Bute sits by the bull's head and praises the noble beast that was, while Sandwich, holding a large basting spoon, comments that there is less fat than before. As leader of the government, Lord North serves as waiter for the nations who have contributed to England's downfall. A Frenchman demands part of the brown; Indian Princess America, knife and fork raised, asks for a portion of the buttock; Spain requests some flank. A Dutchman sits on the floor with a bowl of memorial broth, a reference to the succession of complaints of treaty violations lodged by England against Holland.

The verse beneath comments further:

Behold the poor Bull! once Britania's chief boast,
Is kill'd by State Cooks, and laid down for a Roast:
While his Master, who should all his Honours
  maintain,
Turns the Spit tho' he should such an Office disdain.

Monsieur licks his gills at a bit of the Brown,
And the other two wish for to gobble him down,
But may ill digestion attend on the treat,
And the Cooks every one soon be roasted, & Eat.

B.M. 5636

1960-75

The BULL ROASTED: or the POLITICAL COOKS Serving their CUSTOMERS.

Behold the poor Bull! once Britania's chief boast.
Is kill'd by State Cooks, and laid down for a Roast:
While his Master, who should all his Honours maintain.
Turns the Spit tho' he should such an Office disdain.

Monsieur licks his gills at a bit of the Brown.
And the other two wish for to gobble him down.
But may ill digestion attend on the treat.
And the Cooks every one soon be roasted & Eat.

56. *THE BULL OVER-DROVE: OR THE DRIVERS IN DANGER.*

PUBLISHER: [John Harris][1]
DATE: [February 21, 1780]
SIZE: 7⅞" x 12⅞" (20 cm. x 32.7 cm.)

IN addition to the colonial conflicts the domestic policies of British leaders were bringing the country close to civil war. The satirist suggests that the English bull, shown roasted in the previous satire, can and must be revived. The skillful suggestion is that the bull kick out the unpopular and destructive politicians—North, Sandwich, and Germain. A group of antigovernment onlookers, just behind the bull, rejoices. However, to the right, the allies—France, America, and Spain—view this new, more positive action with alarm because renewed English vigor might result in their defeat.

The verse beneath further comments:

The State Drovers to madness, had drove the poor Bull,
Their Goads and their Tethers no longer can rule,
He Snorts Kicks and Tramples among the curst rout,
Who fall by his Fury or Stagger about.

O! may all such Drovers thus meet with their Fate,
Who Hamper, and Gall so, the Bull of the State,
May his Terror, thus fill them with fear, and dismay,
While the People all Chearfully Cry out, Huzza!

B.M. 5640   1960-76

---

1. The publisher and date have been trimmed from the Colonial Williamsburg impression but are still present on the British Museum copy.

The BULL OVER-DROVE: or the DRIVERS in DANGER.

The State Drovers to madness: had drove the poor Bull.
Their Goads and their Tethers no longer can rule.
He Snorts Kicks and Tramples among the curst rout.
Who fall by his Fury or Stagger about.

O! may all such Drovers thus meet with their Fate.
Who Hamper: and Gall so, the Bull of the State.
May his Terror: thus fill them with fear, and dismay.
While the People all Chearfully Cry out, Huzza!

57. *THE ENGLISH LION DISMEMBER'D*

MAKER: Attributed to Thomas Colley
PUBLISHER: Edward Hedges
DATE: March 12, 1780
SIZE: 9¼″ x 13½″ (33.5 cm. x 34.3 cm.)

IF readers feel that this print has a familiar appearance, they should glance back to No. 5, which has the same title and a similar although not identical picture. While earlier the dismembered lion symbolized the loss of British bases during the French and Indian War, it now represents Revolutionary War losses.

In many of the previous prints England was symbolized primarily as a distraught woman. Hoping to use their influence to defeat present government leaders and alter policies, satirists have returned to a more virile representation that employs John Bull, a real bull, or a lion. Lord North, struggling under the weight of a heavy bag marked "Budget," drags the chained and wounded animal. America, now an Indian chief, holds a staff with the liberty cap and claims the lion's severed paw, "America." Sword in hand, France stands behind the lion ready to sever another limb, while Spain is reluctant to join in the slaughter for fear he will end with nothing. To the right are three members of the opposition party who are determined to stop North before more damage is done to their country.

B.M. 5649

1960-77

126

THE ENGLISH LION DISMEMBER'D
Or the Voice of the Public for an Enquiry into the Public Expenditure.

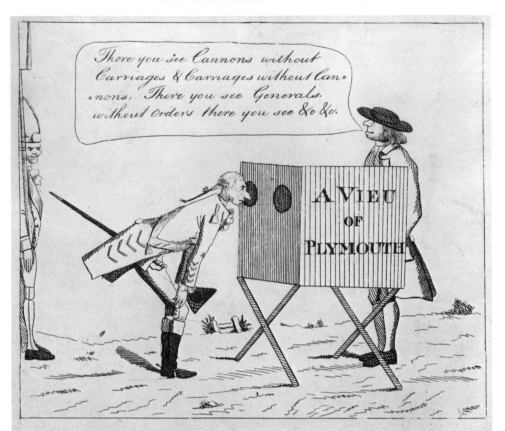

58. *A VIEU OF PLYMOUTH*

PUBLISHER: Matthew Darly
DATE: May 4, 1780
SIZE: 5½″ x 6½″ (14 cm. x 16.5 cm.)

THE peep show, whether drawn elaborately as in No. 51 or simply as here, became an increasingly popular device for satirists to comment on current affairs. Attired in a general's uniform, Lord Jeffrey Amherst bends down to view the show. The operator explains to him: "There you see Cannons without Carriages & Carriages without Cannons. There you see Generals without Orders there you see &c. &c."

A further explanation in the form of a directive appears beneath the picture: "Col. Mushrooms Compts. to Lord Am----t [Amherst] recommends this cheap but Satisfactory mode of viewing distant Garrisons hopes his Lordship has received the Golden Pippins a few of them are for his Secretary."

Amherst was then chief military adviser in the English government. He was under attack for remaining safely in London while faulty, inadequate equipment was dispatched from Plymouth and other ports to the troops in America, thus contributing to further losses in battle. In addition, charges of profiteering had been leveled against Amherst, which the satirist suggests by referring to a particularly fine but scarce apple, the golden pippin.

B.M. 5662   1960-78

59. *ARGUS.*

MAKER: Attributed to James Gillray
PUBLISHER: W. Renegal
DATE: May 15, 1780
SIZE: 9¼″ x 13¼″ (23.5 cm. x 33.6 cm.)

THIS satire attributed to Gillray comments on George III's reluctance to deal effectively with English problems. Fully attired in his royal robes, a sleeping monarch allows government leaders to usurp the symbols of his power.[1] Mansfield, in judge's robe, removes the king's crown. He is observed by the Scotsman Bute, who holds the king's scepter and is aided by a figure whose speech suggest that he is also Scottish, probably Alexander Wedderburn, then attorney general. Observing the scene from the rear is America, a male Indian, who comments: "We in America have no Crown to Fight for or Loose."

Britannia, a despairing female, sits to one side, badly torn maps of Great Britain and America at her feet. The chained British lion sleeps beside her. To the left a ragged unidentified Englishman suggests widespread commercial ruin, while just behind him Ireland walks away declaring his independence.

In the right rear a Dutchman runs away with two bee hives that symbolize the commercial wealth Holland has gained at Britain's expense.

B.M. 5667   1960-79

---

1. The title of the print *Argus* and the sleeping king are a most skillful satiric device. Argus, a Greek mythological figure, was supposed to have a hundred eyes that watched over everything.

ARGUS.

Pub.^d May 18th 1780. by W. Renagal.

60. *THE MAYOR RETURNING THANKS TO LD. AM---T, AT THE SAME TIME HAD THE HONOUR TO KISS AN ASS.*

PUBLISHER: Hannah Humphrey[1]
DATE: About 1780
SIZE: 5″ x 7″ (12.7 cm. x 17.8 cm.)

LORD AMHERST, due to his official government position as military adviser, became the object of much satiric comment in 1779–80. In the peep show (No. 58) the designer rebuked him for commanding the British forces in America from a safe place in London. The attack continues here as he is reproached for his management of a domestic affair.

Among Britain's continuing problems was the religious dispute between Protestants and Catholics in Scotland that threatened to extend into England. Opposed to the removal of many of the long-standing restrictions against Catholicism in Great Britain, the Protestants united against proposed reforms, and riots led by George Gordon broke out in London on June 2, 1780. Amherst called soldiers into the city to quell the fighting. He garrisoned the troops in London in order to avert further trouble, but instead of putting an end to the disturbances their presence actually provoked additional incidents.

In this unsophisticated print the satirist had directed public attention to Amherst's action. Breeches lowered, he stands with his hand on a post inscribed 10,000 £, the amount it supposedly cost to feed the garrisoned troops. Brackley Kennett, lord mayor of the city, stoops to kiss Amherst's exposed bottom in gratitude for his help, instead of protesting the situation. An alderman appropriately attired is next in line.

B.M. 5690   1960-156

---

1. Few women were involved in the making or publishing of political satires. Mary Darly, whose works are represented earlier in this volume, was one. Here Hannah Humphrey, sister of William whose publications also have been shown, joins the feminist ranks. She was to remain an important figure in London publishing circles for the rest of the century.

The Mayor returning thanks to L.d Am——t. at the same time had the honour to kiss an Ass.

Pub by I.Humphrey. No 18 New Bond Street.

61. *RECRUES ANGLOIA PARTANT POUR L'AMÉRIQUE*
(English recruits going to America)

MAKER: Attributed to J. Juillet
PLACE OF PUBLICATION: [France]
DATE: About 1780
SIZE: 10⅛" x 13¼" (25.7 cm. x 33.6 cm.)

A FAVORITE subject for eighteenth-century humorous satires was that of a nondescript group of recruits being processed for army duty. Sometime around 1780 Henry William Bunbury, one of the most skillful of English comic artists, did a rendering of it, and shortly after France allied itself with the American colonies the Bunbury satire was adapted by J. Juillet to comment on the recruitment of French troops for the conflict.

Three motley conscripts have been lined up for inspection in a tavern yard under a sign of a wounded soldier. The inscription "Retour de l'Amérique, Pauvre Fortune" (Back from America, bad luck) presents a very pessimistic picture of what they can expect. Undisturbed by the affair, a young woman is resting against the side of the building mending breeches, presumably for one of the tattered group.

B.M. 4766 (Bunbury version)   1960-70

134

Recrues Angloise partant pour l'Amérique

Angliche Recruts going to America

62. DEN DOOR LIST EN GEWELD AANGEVALLEN LEEUW.

(The lion attacked by cunning and force.)

PLACE OF PUBLICATION: [Holland]
DATE: 1780[1]
SIZE: 7½" x 15½" (19 cm. x 39.4 cm.)

DURING the early Revolutionary War period Holland, disregarding treaties of alliance with England and ostensibly remaining neutral, actually carried on a profitable trade with the colonies and their allies. Many of the previous satires have commented on this. The number of naval skirmishes involving English and Dutch ships increased. Finally England declared war against the Dutch in December 1780 just as Holland was preparing to sign a treaty of armed neutrality with Russia, Sweden, and Denmark. During and immediately following these events unknown Dutch makers issued a series of satires that reflect the somewhat confused sentiments of the populace, who although sympathetic to the colonial cause were fearful of what the war would mean to Holland's favorable economic climate. The next eleven satires are from this group.

The designer has placed caricatures of the nations engaged in the disputes on a rough map of Europe. Each is numbered and a full description is printed below the picture. Included are: (1) Dutch merchants who, although they desire restitution of goods lost during English naval attacks, realize that war with England may endanger their Far Eastern trade. (2) A Stadholder, representing the Dutch king, explains to the merchants that since he has tried to strengthen the nation's defenses, they must not be deluded into taking strong action against others. (3) Sir Joseph Yorke, the British ambassador to Holland, apologizes for the latest attack on Dutch shipping but warns that if they continue to supply arms to the enemy their actions will lead to more conflicts. (4) The Dutch lion, holding in his paw seven arrows symbolic of the United Provinces, has his eyes shielded by the hat of the French ambassador, while (5) an ex-Jesuit takes one arrow. The Frenchman hopes that the blinded animal, Holland, can be brought into the conflict against England; the Jesuit hopes the pope can restore Catholicism in Holland while the country's attention is distracted by other events. (6) Attired in a doublet, Spain points a spear at the Dutch lion. He realizes that although the alliance may prove disadvantageous, it may lead to the return of Gibraltar and give him new power. (7) A Dutch minister of state laments the events that seem to be destroying his country, and (8) another leader watches a convoy bound for Portsmouth and wishes that England and Holland could remain friends so that Dutch vessels would not be converted to fighting ships. (9) A monk is hitched to an elaborate cart decorated with emblems of the Catholic Church. It carries a female, the "Whore of Babylon," an often-used symbol for the church during the eighteenth century. The vignette represents the pope's attempts to regain a foothold in Holland while the country is in conflict with Protestant England.

B.M. 5712   1960-81

---

1. The British Museum impression of this satire is undated. It adds two figures at the top right who continue the discussion of French influences on Holland and its trade.

DEN DOOR LIST en GEWELD AANGEVALLEN LEEUW.

VERKLAARING van de Plaat, en van 't geen elk Personage veronderfteld word te zeggen; dienende tot vervolg op de Brief van CATO-BATAVUS.

In 't verfchiet ziet men aan de eene kant een aanwyzing van de Haven van Breft, en van de Aankomft der Hollandfche *Scheeps-materialen* aldaar; en aan de andere kant een aanwyzing van de Haven van Portsmouth, en van het Hollands Convoy door de Commodore Fielding opgebragt.

(1.) Eenige bekende Kooplieden, met groote drift roepende: *Reftitutie! Satisfactie! ONGELIMI-TEERT CONVOY!* — Dog een van dezelve zig omdrayende, zegt grimlachende: *Wy hebben ondertuf-fen al eenige Capitaaltjes gewonnen; maar 't is evenwel goed te klagen, om de gemoederen te verbitteren, fchoon de Engelfchen 't geen onder ons vals betalen, en een Oorlog met Engeland's grootfte gedeelte onzer Meede-Broeders waarfchynelyk na de grond zal helpen, en onze Bezittingen in de Oeft in gevaar zal ftellen.*

(2.) Z: H: de Kooplieden op de door Lift en Gewelt aangevalle Leeuw wyzende: *Ziet, Mynheeren wat 'er gaande i ; dit heb ik lang voorzien, en daarom, fchoon vrugteloos, getragt de Republik in ftaat van Defenfie te brengen; Wy zyn verlooren, zoo wy ons door drift of looze ftreeken laten mizlyden! Dog ik zal eindelyk genoot-zaakt zyn het Schip te laten dryven.*

(3.) Den Eng: Amb: de Schouders ophalende: *Het Voorval doet my leed; dog ik heb getragt het voor te komen, en cordaat gewaarfchouwt. Het valt hard een Bondgenoot den Vyand, gewapenderhand alles te zien toe-voeren; terwyl men aan Ons het verfchuldigt Secours weigert. Dog de Kogel is nu door de Kerk, en waar-fchynelyk zal het 'er niet by blyven.*

(4.) Den Fr: Amb: de Leeuw met eene hand ftreelende, en met de andere dezelve, compliments-gewys, de Hoed voor de Oogen houdende: *Alles zal wel gaan, zoo ik de Leeuw maar b.ind kan houden, en de Hollanders langzamerhand aan den dans met Engeland kan brengen. O! Wat zullen wy een fchoone Rol fpeelen, als wy by Ons Land-vermogen, de Heerfchappy der Zee gevoegt zullen hebben!*

(5.) Een Ex-Jefuit, volgens de Societeit's Grond-regul; *Divide & impera,* den Band van EENDRAGT los-maakende, en een der Zeven Pylen reets half uit den Bundel getrokken hebbende: *Dat gaat goed! — Als een* PATRIOT *vermomd, zal 't my wel gelukken den Leeuw ongemerkt eenige Pylen te ontfutfelen, en dan mag de* PAUS *onze Order wel herftellen; zoo de Hollanders, die zoo gemakkelyk niet te bedotten zyn als onze goe-de Spagnaards; maar geen lont beginnen te ruiken voer dat ons werk voltooit is!*

(6.) Een Spagnaard den Leeuw van agteren aanvallende: *Wie weet of wy nu eindelyk onze oude GEU-SEN nog niet weder onder de knie krygen? — Dog eerft moet Buurman Vrankryk zyn loozen handel voltragt hebben, want wy zyn thans van eene Familie, fchoon dit ons juift nog niet veel voordeel is geweeft. Maar als wy eens Gibraltar zullen te rug hebben, dan zullen wy de andere Mogentheeden fchoon de Wet kunnen voorfchry-ven! — Ondertuffen hebben wy reets een proffje daar van genomen, en de Hollanders eenige terpen gegeeten.*

(7.) Een Staats-Minifter, de verblinde Leeuw met fmert befchouwende: *O! Hemel, waar zal dit alles nog voor het lieve VADERLAND in voleinden! — Dog ik kan niet meer doen als myne ontdekkingen ge-trouw aan den dag te leggen.*

(8.) Een ander Staats-Minifter, na het opgebragt Convoy ziende: *Dat's boos! — Schoon wy van onze kant de Engelfchen ook in zoo wat reden van klagen hebben gegeeten. Het valt moeyelyk twee twiftende Partyen tot Vriend te houden. Dog wat nu gedaan? — Want fchoon door kragt van Toverkunft, ten ge-noege van eenige onzer windrige Poëten, alle onze ügte Fregatten in Drie-Dekkers veranderden, waar halen wy bevaaren Matroozen van daan? — De Noordfche Mogentheeden hebben die zelfs van noden. Ondertuffen zyn wy aan den haak, en zullen het gelach moeten betalen; Waarover Vrankryk ons dan nog dapper zal uitlachen!*

(9.) Een Munnik, op 't gerugt van een Ruptuur tuffchen Engeland en de Republik, vrolyk naar Fol-land ryzende: *Ons oogmerk is berykt, dank onze gevynfde Tolerantie! Dog nu wy de Hollanders met hun oude Bondgenoot gebrouilleert hebben, en de KETTERS onder malkander aan 't grabbelen hebben gebregt, zullen wy het Spel met hun wel weer meefter werden; daar toe breng ik goede Voorraad meede!*

1780.

63. *DE ONTWAAKTE LEEUW*
(The lion awakened)

PLACE OF PUBLICATION: [Holland]
DATE: About 1780
SIZE: 7¾" x 12¾" (19.7 cm. x 32.4 cm.)

MANY of the figures in this satire duplicate those encountered in the previous work, and continue to comment on Continental affairs during the Revolutionary period. Unfortunately the explanation accompanying the print has been trimmed from the Colonial Williamsburg impression, but the British Museum copy retains it and describes the events as follows: (1) The Dutch lion, holding in his paw the seven arrows representative of the United Provinces, displays anger toward the French ambassador (6). (2) The lady wearing an imperial crown represents Catherine the Great of Russia. She holds a ribbon linked to Denmark (13), Sweden (4), and the Dutch lion to symbolize the recently signed treaty of alliance. (5) Realizing that the lion is still alert, the Jesuit knows that hopes for restoration of Catholicism to Holland are slight. (6) The frightened French ambassador decides not to harass the lion further. (7) The English ambassador is in a rage over Holland's refusal to honor past alliances but is chided by (8) the Dutch king, William V, for arbitrary British actions that have caused all the misfortunes. (9) Spain explains to France that Holland's new alliance offers them little help. (10) The cart transporting the "Whore of Babylon" is in retreat and predicts defeat for the attempts to restore Catholicism to Holland.

B.M. 5713

1960-82

DE ONTWAAKTE LEEUW

64. *LOON NA. WERK 1780*
(A due reward 1780)

PLACE OF PUBLICATION: [Holland]
DATE: About 1780
SIZE: 5⅞" x 9⅝" (14.9 cm. x 24.4 cm.)

CONTINUING the Dutch series, England is now symbolized as a large muzzled dog (1) chained to a pole and much abused by its enemies. (2) A Dutchman pinches the animal's tail. (3) Catherine the Great of Russia, holding a caduceus symbolizing trade and supported by recent allies Sweden and Denmark, signifies her desire to protect commerce on behalf of her friend, Holland.[1] (4) A Frenchman beats the dog with his umbrella hoping to encourage the Dutch to similar positive action. (5) Spain raises a tasseled cane against the British dog and, in a gesture of goodwill, places his other hand on the shoulder of America (6) now in the guise of Yankee Doodle Dandy whose weapon is a knotted scourge. This association of Spain and America is somewhat misleading, for Spain was actually reluctant to support colonial independence and

was most often depicted as an observer rather than an active participant unless the action directly involved France. To the rear a half-nude woman, Britannia, described in Dutch as the proud queen of the sea, is flogged by a man attired in naval dress, John Paul Jones. Ships under his command were harassing British naval operations thus pleasing the Dutch who considered him a hero.

B.M. 5715   1960-83

---

1. The earliest symbolic use of a caduceus was as the wand carried by Hermes (or Mercury), messenger of the Gods. It then evolved into a symbol for commerce, and only later was adapted into medical usage.

LOON NA WERK 1780

N.1 Verbeelt Een Engelse Dogge, geketent aan een Ronde Onzydige Paal N.2 Een Hollander alvorens door hem in 't been gebeten zynde let hem een Knip op de Staart, Geadsisteerdt
Door de Neütraliteyt N.3 aan 't Hooft voorzel ve Een Gekroonde Vorstin, edel moedig den Vryen Handel Beschermunde N.4 een Franseman den Hont afreetende Couragerende den Hollander hem
Vryende op zyn Vrienden N.5 Een Spanjaart Met zyn Rotting den Rebel Deftig Strelende en den Amerikaan N.6 aanmoedigt die den Menscheplaag Zapper voor zyn brutale Muyl Slaaët

In 't Verschiet ziet Men de Hoogmoedige Koningin der zee wordende gigeeselt door J. poül Jones

65. *DE MAN IN 'T HEMBD, OF DE GEFNUIKTE HOOGMOED.*
(The man in the shirt or pride brought low.)

PLACE OF PUBLICATION: [Holland]
DATE: About 1780
SIZE: 6¾″ x 8⅔″ (17.1 cm. x 22 cm.)

THE pictorial discussion of the newly ratified treaty of neutrality continues in this Dutch satire. All of the countries are represented by male figures. (1) Distraught England, wearing only a ragged shirt, is held by Denmark (4) and Sweden (5). (7) France puts a fool's cap on England's head while Russia (3), distinguished by a fur hat and long gown, threatens him with a large club. America (2), pleased with the response of other nations, flees with England's clothes, as (6) Holland kneels on the ground to shackle his ankles.

The seashore setting allows the designer to comment on the continuing trade problems. (8) England's loss of trade is indicated by a number of ships aground while (9) shows a fleet in full sail, the commerce that the armed neutrality treaty should allow the allies. (10) An unhappy merchant, probably English, stands on the shore in a gesture of despair. (11) Treaties no longer observed lie torn on the ground.

B.M. 5716   1960-84

142

DE MAN IN 'T HEMBD, OF DE GEFNUIKTE HOOGMOED.

VERKLARING. 1. EEN MAN IN 'T HEMBD, IN VOLLE RAZERNY. 2. EEN AMERIKAAN, DIE LACHENDE ZYN BEURS EN KLEDEREN WEGDRAAGT. 3. EEN MUSKOVIETER DREIGENDE HEM TE SLAAN. 4 EN 5. EEN DEEN EN ZWEED HEM DE ARMEN VASTHOUIENDE. 6. EEN HOLLANDER DIE HEM AAN DE KETTING LEGT. 7. EEN FRANSCHMAN HEM EEN ZOTSKAP OPZETTENDE. 8. EENIGE AFGETAKELDE KAPERS. 9. EEN VLOOT KOOPVAARDY-SCHEPEN ONGESTOORD VARENDE. 10. EEN MAN DIE DIT STAMPVOETENDE AANZIET. 11. EENIGE VERSCHEURDE TRAKTATEN.

66. *DEN BRITSEN LEOPARD TOT REDEN GEBRACHT.*
(The British leopard brought to reason.)

PLACE OF PUBLICATION: [Holland]
DATE: About 1780
SIZE: 9″ x 13⅜″ (22.9 cm. x 34 cm.)

A CHANGE of allegorical symbolism occurs in this group of Dutch prints. When depicted individually both Holland and England have been shown as lions. Now both countries are often shown simultaneously in these satires; Holland remains a lion while England is represented by a leopard.

The explanation has been removed from the Colonial Williamsburg impression but the British Museum copy still retains it and identifies the numbered figures as follows: (1) A Dutchman, his pro-English sentiments explained by papers protruding from his pockets that indicate he has London investments, addresses the two angry beasts, England (2) the leopard and Holland (3) the lion. The man wants them to make peace in the best interest of all. The leopard is clawing at the lion which, although stunned, rises under the protection of a group led by Catherine the Great of Russia (6) who has encircled her allies (7–10), Sweden, Denmark, Prussia, and a maid holding a liberty hat over the united group. (11) Yorke, the English ambassador, tries to sever the circle but is restrained by the French ambassador (12). Standing just behind the animals an Englishman (4) holds a trident from which a chain reaches upward to Lisbon. Although an ally of Britain, Portugal was about to join the alliance of neutrality. (5) A Dutch merchant holds a paper with abbreviated references to former English territory now in the possession of others.

Above this almost procession-like grouping are three single figures. (13) The king of Spain points downward to the word "Florida," an English possession captured by his troops. (14) In a similar gesture France indicates its takeover of Grenada, St. Vincent, and Dominique, while holding in his right hand the liberty hat over North America (15), who sits on bales of much desired goods that are protected by a cannon muzzle. She holds in one hand arrows representing the thirteen colonies, a transfer of symbolism from the United Provinces in the previous satires.

B.M. 5719   1960-85

145

67. [ERWARDIGEN NEDERLANDER]
[Worthy Dutchman]

PLACE OF PUBLICATION: [Holland]
DATE: About 1780
SIZE: 10″ x 15″ (25.4 cm. x 38.1 cm.)

THIS satire is more complex in design than most in the period 1775–80, and a number of elements are reminiscent of those found in the French and Indian War prints shown in the first part of the volume. Again, unfortunately the Colonial Williamsburg impression lacks the explanation, but the British Museum records that it was published as a separate pamphlet, and therefore no direct reference numbers are attached to the figures.

Returning to the well-populated seashore for a setting, the satirist has centered attention on a wealthy Dutchman, his money chest open in front of him. Just behind him a group of Dutch laborers are waiting to be paid. To the left several foreigners, led by a Frenchman and including an Englishman holding alliance treaties, bow in respect and with humble gestures indicate their desire for a share of the Dutch wealth, but receive only scorn.

To the far left three men converse before a chest inscribed "Oeconomische Brillen" (economic glasses) symbolic of the desire of all Dutchmen for greater economic gains.

Behind the Dutch laborers a woman attired in the dress of victory leads a group of colonial sympathizers toward a temple, one pillar of which is being replaced by a number of tiny figures. Within a statue with staff and cap represents liberty.

Above the temple a radiant cloud formation holds six allegorical figures. Five can be identified as the virtues: piety, truth, love, faith, and steadfastness.

In the right foreground a lion, Holland, attacks England, now in the form of a frightened dog, who is already under seige by the cock, France.

Dutchmen had long been investing funds in English banks, but the present political crisis made such ventures unwise. The satirist suggests that even though the English would prefer to have such investments continue, the Dutch might be wiser to invest elsewhere, particularly within the alliance or in their own country.

B.M. 5720

1960-86

146

68. [*HET TEGENWOORDIG VERWARD EUROPA*]

[*Europe in her present disordered state*)

PLACE OF PUBLICATION: [Holland]
DATE: About 1780
SIZE: 10¼″ x 11⅛″ (26 cm. x 28.3 cm.)

AN ancient stone arch from which weeds protrude forms the unusual border of this Dutch print. As in the previous satire attention is focused on the economic hardship suffered by both English and Dutch banking interests as a result of the open declaration of war between the two nations. The financial losses were further intensified by naval harassments and blockades of strategic ports that hampered trade.

Dominating the center of the print is a large chest suspended on a chain from the horn of a unicorn, whose head and torso emerge from a cloud formation. The chest serves as a symbolic scale weighted against an obese Englishman who is about to fall to the ground. His balance is further jeopardized by a Frenchman on the ground who tugs on his leg while an Indian child, America, pushes the man closer to the edge. Behind France an injured Spaniard with a crutch is unable to provide aid. Only a Dutchman, shown on the other side of the chest, prevents total collapse as he holds the leg of the slipping Englishman, meanwhile discussing the situation with another merchant who has an account book. Scattered around the two men are objects representing Dutch trade—cheese, textiles, gold, and so forth—that cannot

be exported. To the rear a pastoral scene further suggests the importance of farm products in Holland's economic life.

Two verses, one in English, the other in Dutch, further comment on the problem:

Bold *Jack!* pray, what's the business to-day?
Phoo--! pox--! a plot, mistaken for a play.
This hurly-burly spoils your sport--! you'll find,
There's humour to your face--, and more behind.
Amazing Fool--! yet tottering on thy bench,
Tho' scorn'd by *Spain*, and cozen'd by the *French*--.
Only the *Dutch*, not laughing at your nose,
Good-natur'd helps, to snatch what-e'er you lose.

Hoezee! tienduizendmaal! van dikhout zaagt men
 deelen.
'tGaat wel: by kris en kras! dat heet een hoofdrol
 speelen.
Puf Spaansch en Fransch: Messieurs! die poen heeft
 maakt figuur.
Maar lieve *Jack*! zie toe: dat stomlen staat je duur.
ô Boston! Delaware! ô Washington! ô Franschen!
Zo Mogt Mylord welhaast een hangmans hornpyp
 danssen.
De Batavier houdt noch uw Bankspel in den haak.
Vermeetle! Loon die trouw, of vrees geregte wraak.

[However much ten thousand times! from thick
 wood one saws pieces.
It does well: criss and cross! that hotheads play a
 leading part.
Fie Spanish & French: Messieurs this vulgar one
 hath made a figure
But Dear Jack! Have a look: That stumbling state you
 endure
O Boston! Delaware! O Washington! O France!
So might Mylord soon dance a hangman's hornpipe.
The Batavian still holds your bank on the square
Do you dare! Reward this faithfully or fear revenge.]

B.M. 5721A   1960-87

Bold *Jack!* pray, what's the business to-day?
Phoo-! pox-! a plot, mistaken for a play.
This hurly-burly spoils your sport-; you'll find,
There 'shumour to your face-, and more behind.
Amazing Fool-! yet tottering on thy bench,
Tho' scorn'd by *Spain*, and cozen'd by the *French*--,
Only the *Dutch*, not laughing at your nose,
Good-natur'd helps, to snatch what-e'er you lose.

Hoezee! tienduizendmaal! van dikhout zaagt men deelen.
't Gaat wel: by kris en kras! dat heet een hoofdrol speelen.
Puf Spaansch en Fransch! Messieurs! die poen heeft maakt figuur.
Maar lieve *Jack!* zie toe: dat stomlen staat je duur.
ô Boston! Delaware! ô Washington! ô Franschen!
Zo mogt Mylord welhaast een hangmans hornpyp danssen.
De Batavier houdt noch uw Bankspel in den haak.
Vermeetle! Loon die trouw, of vrees geregte wraak.

69. *ENGELSCH NIEUWS.*
(English news.)

PLACE OF PUBLICATION: Holland
DATE: About 1780
SIZE: 9″ x 12½″ (22.9 cm. x 31.7 cm.)

AS in the previous work the designer has set this satire on the seashore and has heightened the dramatic effect by utilizing storm clouds and celestial beings. (1) A Dutch sailor holds a paper of complaints and suggests that the English become better acquainted with Holland's present policies. He feels that all of his countrymen should support the embargo against British trade instead of a few surreptitiously trading with the enemy. (2) A man in clerical attire, symbolic of Dutch commerce, stands beside a large locked chest containing money. He advises the Dutch to protect their rights without inciting Britain to further action. (3) Mercury, now firmly established as the representative of commerce, pledges to help the Dutch even if to do so might be dangerous.

England is represented by a group on the left. (4) George III, in a long cloak, addresses (5) Lord N**** (North) concerning England's increasing troubles. (6) Lord Shelburne, a prominent member of the Opposition, stands with his back to the others as he examines a picture of religious riots (then prevalent in Britain) that is inscribed "Het verwar de Eiland" (Distracted Island). England's problems have become so serious that its leaders cannot resolve them.

(7) A tall figure represents Lord George Gordon, leader of the anti-popery riots. He proclaims his belief that the upsurge of Catholicism in England must be stopped even if violent action is necessary.

The figures in the cloud are victory, wearing a helmet and holding a picture of a ship, the Dutch lion who carries a staff with a liberty cap, and peace with a wreath and a globe on her head. This prophetic scene features black clouds over the English, the figures of peace and victory over Holland, and lightning about to strike Gordon.

A sea battle is raging in the background, while soldiers fight on the distant shore. One has already fallen.

B.M. 5722   1960-88

150

ENGELSCH NIEUWS.

No. 1. *Een Hollander; al wederom met Nieuwe Klachten naer London. De Engelschen moesten ons beter kennen; wy zelve weten best, wat ons te doen staat; Koopbandel en Staatkunde waren altoos ons gezelschap; ik twyffel niet, of de dagelyksche geweldenaryen zullen op schade der daders uitkomen.*

2. *Staatkunde, klaag onophoudelyk; verget niet het schenden onzer Kusten en Scheepen ten sterksten voor te dragen; houd uwen Vriend Mercurius ter deege vast; door hem zyt gy overal welkom, en zoo lang by by u blyft zult gy nodig en ontzien zyn, door alle uwe nageburen; want daar een ieder derzelver hem gaarne onder zyne Macht zag, zal altoos de andere oog in het zeil bewaren. Het zoude voor een Leeuw schande zyn, niet eens te brullen, als men hem zoo ten onrecht de Lokken uittrekt. — Het is onvoorzichtig, daar by in redelykheid iets toegeeft, hem te tergen, om dat men weet dat zyne Natuur Edelmoedig is.*

3. *Mercurius; zoo lang gy een recht Hollander blyft, zal ik u niet verlaten, by u ben ik best; want myn aart is meerder voor my zelven, dan voor een ander te zorgen; uwe geduurige naarstigheid, uwe onderneemendheid, en beredeneerde, schoon langzame, geestigheid, kan my doen bloeijen, schoon het tegenwoordig vry gevaarlyke tyden voor my zyn; maar waar kan ik thans de bestendige rust genieten, zonder genoodzaakt te zyn, eens uit myn Celletje van myn Reekenboek op te staan, om myne gedachten en oogen op ruimer Velden uit te breiden.*

4. *Een zeer voornaam Engelschman; ach! myn lieve Lord, wat nu? Laat uwe oogen eens op dit nog niet volkomene afgewerkte Tafereel weiden; beroerte binnen en buiten verteeren ons.*

5. *Lord N****, laat ons deeze beete Koorts, waar van 't ingewand des Ryks trild, zoo het erger wil, op denzelven voet, gelyk die Schotze zaaken behandelen, willig, maar, in het geene zy willen. — Wel is het, zoo wy het thans als Meesters kunnen toestaan; maar laat de woorden; wyl wy het thans dienstig vinden, vooral niet uit, — wy moeten den oorspronk, willen wy meerder gevaar ontgaan, thans maar van verre kennen — dat 'er by provisie een belooning van 500 Ponden op de ontdekking van den Dader of Daders werd gesteld; maar wegens de buitelandsche onlusten, wat zullen wy met de Hollanders beginnen? hunne klachten, vrees ik, zyn niet ongegrond; gelukkig zoo 'er een onder ons is, die de geparte middelen uitvindt; wy wachten veel van Lord Shelburne — maar ongelukkig is 'er een Hertog onpasselyk, en daar door word een plan om zaaken van gewicht zoo dra mogelyk af te doen, te rug gebou-*

den. Onze Marine diend ook eens overzien te worden; Rodny schryft veel, maar wat baat een overwinning, die niets beslist; dagelyks wagten wy het Fregat met Officieren, wier gedrag onderzoek vordert; welhaast zal het ons zoo veel moeite kosten om Kapteins, als Matroosen te doen; doch deze taak kunnen Lord Sandwich en de overigen afbaspelen. De Hemel, hoop ik, Zegene hun en ons allen.

No. 6. *Lord Shelburne; wat is het zwaar beladen te gaan met een zwaarte, die de gantsche Natie verlichten moet; iedere nieuwe gebeurtenis maakt inbreuk op myne ontwerpen; de Hollanders heffen sterker hunne klagende, en, nu eenigzints dreigende toonen aan. De Franschen hebben thans sterken invloed op dat Land; zy stremmen hunnen Koopbandel niet, nog neemen hunne Scheepen niet, en wy gaan wat verre, voor Vrienden, en wat meerder is, voor Bondgenooten.*

7. *Lord Gordon; wel begonnen, maar nog niet voleindigd, zoude die hoogen vloed der genegenheid van het driftig Gemeen niet in een laage ebbe verkeeren kunnen, en wat dan met Gordon? Het past geen Edelman van zyn stuk af te staan; men moge vry zeggen, wat begint dat dweepend heethoofd? Zoo by het wel meent; waarom zyne Vaderland in zulk een knellenden tyd met nieuwe inlandsche onlusten en rampen overstroomd? Dit is de weg van een Dwaas; en zoo by zulks niet is, moet by zeeker een Guit zyn; wyl die op zyn luimen lag, om in een tyd, voor andere bezigheden geschikt, eene Edelmoedige zaak, die nimmer onrust of verwarring gaf, door geweld en mishandeling zyner medevaderlanders om te werpen; — maar die dit zeggen, gelieven te weeten, dat onze Godsdienst my na aan het harte ligt, schoon veele zedekundige regelen, gelyk onder andere die, hebt uwe Vyanden lief, vermaan uwen Broeder, in overtuiging en zagtzinnigheid des harten, enz. my ter beoeffening wel wat meerder moeite kosten — om den sterken invloed der Catholyke Leer tegen te gaan, wilde ik wel eene vraag, een verzoek, door myn byzyn ondersteunen, maar wie wist, dat de drift zoo ver zoude gaan? dat mishandelen, dat in brand steeken, 't is waaragtig alles buiten my. — Geloof niet, dat ik, die de zuivre Leer van nedrigheid ombels, in myn hart zoo verre myne reede verbasteren kan, om alom myn Naam te doen rond bazuinen, al zoude het my alles kosten, gelyk die dwaas, door het afbranden des Epheezischen Tempels zogt; neen, veel liever tot heil, tot verzagting en troost myner medeburgeren is al myn wensch; — konden myne handen die wonden heelen, welken die onvoorzigtigheid der Tveerzaten aan myne waarde medeburgers heeft toegebragt, zy zouden 'er niet meer zyn. Ach! dat wy alle als Lammeren, en niet als Wolven, in de Schaapskudde waaren.*

70. *DE WANHOOPIGE BRITTEN, EN DE VERNOEGDE AMERICANEN*
(The despairing Briton, and the contented America)

PLACE OF PUBLICATION: [Holland]
DATE: [About 1780]
SIZE: 6½″ x 4½″ (16.5 cm. × 11.4 cm.)

A small picture is placed between two lengthy columns that discuss the complex relationship between England and Holland during this period of the Revolution. In this Dutch satire the figures are numbered and explained in the text.

(1) George III is seated before an array of playing cards, broken china, and papers as he contemplates empty money bags. He admits that had England dealt more tolerantly with America, the Treasury might now be intact. (2) Appearing anxious, North comments on the damage done England by the Continental neutrality pacts as he slowly comprehends his mistakes in policy.

(3-6) Dutchmen converse about the present difficult economic situation. (3) A merchant brags about successful smuggling operations while acknowledging the damage caused by British sea operations. (4) A manufacturer displays his superior Dutch cloth and worries that trade has declined because of the conflict. (5) A dejected merchant complains that ships have been captured and goods have been confiscated by the British.

(7 and 8) Two Spaniards discuss the decline of their country.

(9 and 10) A French designer displays a painting of animals that illustrate the fables of La Fontaine and speculates on their double meanings to a long-gowned Dutch philosopher.

To the rear a cannon is fired from a fortress at ships in the harbor. (11) Sitting on a small scale, a male Indian, America, is content to merely observe arguments between France, Spain, Holland, and England, but is filled with praise for the new neutrality treaty. (12 and 13) Two figures, Balsepf and Jersey, pack barrels of trade goods ready for delivery to their mother country, England, as soon as peace can be restored.[1]

B.M. 5724

1960-92

---

1. These figures represent two of England's possessions. The Channel Island of Jersey had recently been under attack from the French, who threatened its trade. The reference to Balsepf, which is probably intended to represent Belfast, Ireland, is more obscure. This country too had been threatened with curtailment of trade because of the war, but in 1780 England allowed the resumption of shipments both to the colonies and to other British possessions.

DE WANHOOPIGE BRITTEN, en de VERNOEGDE AMERICANEN, op de TYDING

van DIFFENSIVE ALLIANTIE, ONBEPAALT CONVOY, en GEWAPENDE NEUTRALITEIT!

Verklaaring van de Nevensstaande KUNST PLAAT, zoo als de Perzoonen hier volgens de Nommer Verbeeld worden te Spreeken.

1. GEORGE GARTHER een der *aanzienlykste Engelschen*, in een bedrukte en allerbeklaaglykste houding Leunende met het Hoofd in de s'Linkerhand, te gelyk zig agter het oor klauwende en met een verslagen gezigt ziende op de Leedig geworodene Geldzakken en de Gezeegelde Papieren der onlangs gedaane Negotiatien; by zig zelve uitroepende, Ach! hadden wy wat meer *Tolerant* gehandeld met onze Broederen de *Americaanen*, wy hadden zoo onnoemlyke Schatten niet door een nutteloozen Oorlog verkwist, en de *Engelsche* Natie in zulke onbetaalbaare schulden niet gestooken; maar heelaas! nu zitten wy 'er deerlyk meden in 't naauw, en ik ben ten einde raadt.

2. EEN voornaame ENGELSCHE LORD, in een allerdifperaadste gestalte de Oogen opwaards heffende, en de handen al Bevende te samenvoegende; zich op een wanhoopige wyze beklagende en by zig zelve uitroepende, ô die neutraliteit! die neutraliteit! die *diffensive Alliantie*! van Rusland, Sweeden, Deenmarken, Portugal, de Vereenigde Nederlanden en alle de Hanze steeden! ô die neutraliteit! die maakt het ons te benaauwt, waar zal het nu met ons heen? ô Elendige *Engelsche*, hoe zal het noch met u afloopen? al schoon dat de Koogel nu door de Kerk scheen te zyn, ik vrees, ik vrees! vyf a ses duyzend NOORDSCHE MATROOZEN! en dan noch vyftien of twintig wel bemande RUSSISCHE OORLOGSCHEEPEN! ô GARTHER GARTHER! Nu begin ik eerst regt benaauwt en bekommert te worden, ik voorzie nu klaar dat men het Schip niet zal laaten dryven, zoo als op de Plaat van den door list en geweld aangevallene Leeuw door No. 2. voorfpelt wat te doen.

3. EEN HOLLANDSCHE *Koopvaardy Schipper*, zittende op een *Baal Zeyldoek*, en verhaalende met een vernoegt gezigt, aan den Koopman No. 5. en aan den Fabrikeur No. 4. de oplettende toe hooren, verscheide smokkel Partytjes, die door hem en andere in voorige tyden, en nu in deze troeble omstandigheeden ook noch verrigt zyn; benevens eenige wreede en onbillyke behandelingen aan hem gepleegt door de *Engelsche Kaapers*, alles meest onder schyn van Americaanen, gevende ten dien einde aan de Fabrikeur No. 4. een gedrukt Boekje, genaamt *de Spiegel der Jeugds of de Britsche Tiranny*, het welk hy den *Fabrikeur* op een behendige wyze by de borst in steekt, zeggende leest; leest my vrient wat de Engelsche niet voor braave Bondgenooten en goede Vrienden van onzen staat zyn; zie hier in dit boekje, wat de Hollanders voor fraije ontmoetingen met haare Vrienden en Helaas! Bondgenooten niet algehadt hebben.

4. EEN HOLLANDSCHE FABRIKEUR, een hollandsch Laaken vertoonende aan No. 3. De Koopvaardy Schipper, en aan No. 5. den Koopman; hun lieden de waare deugd van het Hollandsche, in tegen overstelling van het Engelsche Aantoonende; en zich zeer beklagende over het verval der *Fabriken* in ons Vaderland, en over de geringe Negotie en Verzendingen in *Hollandsche Manufactuuren*; te gelyk niet veel goeds verhaalende van de Engelsche, ten opzigten der onderkruipinge in onze *Fabriken*, en het behendige afhaalen van onze *Contante Penningen*, door aanlokkende Negotiatien, en behaaglyke en Prompt betaalende de zwaare interesten.

5. EEN HOLLANDSCH KOOPMAN in een bedrukte Houding, gevende te kennen aan de Koopvaardy Schipper No. 3. en aan de Fabrikeur No. 4. dat hy in deze troeble tyden nog geen goede Beurs heeft gemaakt zoo als veel van zyne Confraters wel doen, en dat het in een beroerd water goed te vissen is, zulks werd door hem nader verklaard, door een verhaal van die Hollandsche Koopvaardy Scheepen, die onlangs in de *Haven van Brest* zyn aangeland, en het *Hollandsche Convoy*

van den HEERE GRAVE VAN BYLAND, vooruit of onzylt waeren, en dus de oplettenheid van den *Engelsche Comodore Fielding* ter regter tydt zyn ontsnapt; daar de andere in tegendeel zyn opgebragt, waar over hy, en andere Reders, Asfuradeurs, Factoors, Boekhouders, Schippers &c. &c &c. zig onlangs by Requesten zeer beklaagden, daar de anderen die vry en onverhindert vaaren, zig over verheugen, en in middels een goede Beurs maaken en zich Spek vet Meiten.

6. EEN HOLLANDSCHE, *Genever* en *Brandewyn Stooker*, stootende de Koopvaardy Schipper No. 3. met een volle vles Vaderlandsche Schiedamsche Genever aan den arm, hem vragende, of hy GEORGE GARTHER en DEN LORD N...., ook eens Vaderlandsche drank wilde aanbieden, dewyl hy ziet dat zy beiden zoo bekommert en verslaagen scheinen, (en niet anders uitroepen als) ô die *Neutraliteit* ! ô die jes duizend *Noormannen als Matroosen op Zee*! en dan Helaas! twintig *Russische Oorlogscheepen*, en mooglyk noch wel twintig daar by! zoo het eerste niet wel voldoende was, daar hy nu niet twyfeld of die Vaderlandsche drank, zal hen tegenwoordig beeter kragt aan de Ribben zetten dan de opregtste *Engelsche Rum*, of de Origineele *London Porter*, die de Hollanders, doch nimmer met een zuivere smaak gedronken hebben.

7. EEN SPAANSCHE DON, en 8 een SPAANSCHE DUC, beyde op de voorgrond zittende en scheinende in eene ernstige Samenspraak te zyn over het *Noodlot van Spanjen*, zoo wel in de tegenwoordige als voorgaande tyden; en zich beklagende over het gedrag der Spanjaarden ten allen tyden gehouden, en over de geleedene Schaadens, die geduurende in de laatste oorloogen, de Spaansche zyn toegebragt, zoo als in de laastledene oorlog met Engeland klaar gebleeken is; daar het die Moogendheid; Namentlyk de Spaansche, een goede Goudmyn kosten, zonder dat 'er noch eenige glory behaald was, ten kosten van het verspillen van onnoemlyke Schatten: beklaagende zig No. 7. nu niet meer over het voorgaande; maar wel over het onlangs voorgevallene met de Vlootvoogden *Rodney* en *Don Langara*, in den Zeeflag by *Gibralter*, (dat *Groote Appeltje* van verschil) tussen Spanjen en Engeland, dit veroorzaakte by deze Don, en Duc, eene vertwyfelende onderhandeling, om wel ernstiglyk te overweegen wat hen in dezen en in 't vervolg staat te doen; en hoe zy in alle deze omstandigheeden zich zullen gedraagen.

9. EEN FRANSCHE *Project maaker*, laatende aan No. 10. (*een vroome en zedige Hollandsche Philosooph*) eene Schildery zien, waar op eenige der fabelen van de Fransche *de la Fontaine* zyn afgebeeld en uitgeschildert, als die van de *Aap en de Katt*, de *Vos* en de *Aap*, de *Leeuw* en de *Beer*, &c. &c. &c.; waar over zich den *Philosooph* zeer scheint te verwonderen! gevende met zyne Regter hand, zyne verwondering, en met zyne s'Linkerhand op het Hart drukkende; zyne bekommering over deze dubbelzinnige fabelen aan den *Franschen Projectmaaker* te kennen.

11. MASSINA RAMBY, een *Americaan*, staande in een vernoegt gelaat, op een zekere afstand de woelingen der Engelschen, Fransche, Spanjaarden &c. &c. &c. met opmerking te beschouwen, en by zig zelve spreekende over het voorzigtig, bezadigt, en Wys gedrag van H. H. M. en Pryzende in zig zelve de stipte en Loflyke Neutraliteit van de VADEREN DES VADERLANDS, in de verschillen tussen *Engeland*, *Frankryk*, *Spanjen*, en *America*, tot dus verre zorgvuldig gehouden.

12 en 13. *Baljeff* en *Jersey*, twee kundige en ervaarne *Americaanen*, te samen wel vergenoegt en ieverig voortvaarende, om de voortbrengselen van hun land, zorgvuldig in te zamelen, te Pakken, af te zenden en scheep te bezorgen; tegenwoordig zig niet bekommerende over hun verdoold Moederland; maar wel te Vreden met hunne aanstaande onafhangelykheid, en de Vrije Koophandel die zy in 't vervolg hoopen te zullen deelagtig worden, onder de Protectie van Vrankryk, — ik hoop dat zy zich door den tyt daar niet in zullen bedrogen zien; het zou my van die braave menschen van harten leed doen.

71. *DAN ONDER DAN BOOVEN.*
(Under and over.)

PLACE OF PUBLICATION: [Holland]
DATE: About 1780
SIZE: 8⅛" x 10½" (20.6 cm. x 26.6 cm.)

DEPARTING slightly in subject matter from the previous Dutch satires in the series, this print makes no comment on the armed neutrality treaty and instead suggests that Holland should consider war with England. The numbered figures are explained in the text at the bottom.

(1) Father Time turns a wheel of fortune upon which four figures attempt to stay in balance. England, on the right, is engaged in a fight with America, and France appears dangerously close to falling from the wheel. To the left, Spain is watching the struggle without offering help.

(2 and 3) Two Dutchmen stand beside the wheel, one dressed as a sailor, the other as a statesman. His patience ending, the sailor demands action to restore Holland's favorable trade position. The statesman pleads for restraint.

(4) A monk points across the ocean to the burning city of London, also observed by (5) a Protestant. Both lament the religious riots that have caused such distress in England.

B.M. 5725

1972-83
PROVENANCE: The Old Print Shop

DAN ONDER DAN BOOVEN.

No. 1. Den tyd het wankelbaar Rad des Oorlogs in een geduriglyke beweging houdende, en thans den Engelsman weder een weinig boven draaijende, het welk oorzaak is dat den Franschman, Americaan en Spanjaart rykelyk wat met hem te doen hebben, en van den forschen Engelsman eenige suffisante slagen profiteeren, *wild gy tegens een Engelsman Kampen? Dan bedriegt gy u zelfs, wy moeten nog over de gantsche Wereld heerschen, en daarom is ons 't zelfde of wy Vrienden dan Vyanden hebben.*

2. Een Jongen Fluksschen Hollander, vragende om restitutie van zyn geleden schaaden, *indien gy Mylord my niet schadeloos houd in myn Eer en Goed zal ik eens zien of ik altoos van u zal onderdrukt worden. Gelooft dat myn geduld ten einde loopt en al was gy dan nog zoo Hoogmoedig, weet dat veel Honden den Haas zyn dood zyn, en gy ten langen lesten u wel zoude kunnen berouwen. Ik stel het u nogmaals voor.......*

3. Een Voorzigtigen Staatsman den Hollander zagtjes by den schouder trekkende, *Bedaar! Bedaar Broer, en vraagt niet meer te vergeefs om restitutie, schei uit met Memorien in te leveren, wilt gy schade vergoeding hebben? Wel aan Wapent u, en verschaft u zelve Regt; ik heb alles in 't werk gesteld om dien Hoogmoedigen de gevaren onder 't oog te brengen, dog te vergeefs, het zyn Engelschen: maar laten wy nu toonen dat wy Hollanders zyn.*

No. 4. Een Monnik zyn gezigt naar Londen wendende, *ziet, die dolle Ketters eens Huishouden, dat is onverdraaglyk! Ach Roomsche Mogendheden! is dat om aan te zien? Straft zulke Kerk-Schenners, wat zal anders het einde zyn?*

5. Een Protestant den Munnik bedarende, *maak zo veel gerugts niet myn Vriend, ik schaam my zelve over de schandelykheid van dit doen. Maar die zyn eige Koning niet ontziet het Hoofd af te slaan, zullen die haar ontzien hunnen Medeburgeren geweld aan te doen? Het is enkelde dweepzugt en muitery, en voor zulk schuim van Volk kan men zig niet wagten, ook zal men haast zien welk een heerlyk loon zy ontvangen zullen.*

72. *VERKLAARING.*
(Explanation)

PLACE OF PUBLICATION: [Holland]
DATE: About 1780
SIZE: 7¼″ x 11⅜″ (18.4 cm. x 28.9 cm.)

THIS satire, whose title is the Dutch word for explanation, depicts Holland's reaction to George III, Lord North, and Oliver Cromwell, the English leaders whose policies contributed to difficult relations between the two countries. The references are explained as follows: (1) Seated on his throne, George III is being undressed by two young men whose feathered caps identify them as Americans. He calls for help from North (2), who, riding on an old nag, seems unlikely to reach the king in time to aid him. (3) On a pedestal inscribed "Uytvinder van Heersch en baatzugt" (inventor of ambition and covetness) is a bust of Oliver Cromwell. Three English admirers kneel before it oblivious to justice emerging from the clouds holding in one hand thunderbolts with which to strike them down. Cromwell was held responsible for the navigation acts in the mid-seventeenth century that first curtailed free trade in England and became to the Dutch a symbol for any threat to commerce. Ironically, however, the figure wears a sixteenth-century Tudor cap suggesting that the bust is of Thomas Cromwell, a religious leader, and not of Oliver. By this touch the satirist suggests that the English would bow to anyone with the name Cromwell.

B.M. 5729   1960-91

VERKLAARING.

73. [*YORK TOWN*]

PLACE OF PUBLICATION: [Holland]
DATE: About 1781[1]
SIZE: 8½″ x 11¼″ (21.6 cm. x 28.6 cm.)

A DUTCH satirist set this scene at Yorktown, site of the final battle and surrender of the Revolutionary War. Liberally borrowing symbols from other published works, the maker also took much of the foreground from the popular English satire *A Picturesque View of the State of the Nation for February 1778* (No. 41), which had been copied later in Holland. To the left the emaciated cow, English commerce, shorn of one horn, grazes on the barren shore. A Spaniard leans on a post inscribed Mexico, Peru, and Chile, three of Spain's few remaining colonial holdings. A Frenchman and Dutchman holding a bowl and a heavy pail gesture toward America to indicate their hopes for the future.

To the right an Englishman kneels in despair beside the British lion, who holds up a paw injured on the broken American teapot lying before him. Rats carry small bank notes, all that remains of the British Treasury, from a broken chest.

The surrender at Yorktown is shown in the rear. Under a tent Indian Princess America sits on a bale of valuable trade goods. In a gesture of peace she holds an unstrung bow in one hand while the other is outstretched toward the approaching British and Scots. Surrounding her are loyal supporters and allegorical figures including Justice and Truth. An Indian seals large barrels labeled "Kadix," "Nantes," and "Marseille" as he prepares to resume trade with the Continent, but there is nothing for England. The wrecked British ship *Eagle* lies half aground in the water; the French fleet is ready to sail once again.

This popular satire was published in several editions: the Dutch shown here, a second without explanation, and a larger impression.

B.M. 5859   1960-96

------

1. This satire is placed very slightly out of chronological sequence in order to retain the Dutch satires as a group.

N.º 2.

VERKLARING DER STAATKUNDIGE PRINT-VERBEELDING, N.º 2.

Wegens de Staat der ENGELSCHE NATIE, in 't Jaar 1773.

1. Een *Engelschman*, in Rouw-gewaad, om 's Hemels bystand smeekende.

2. De ontwaakte *Britsche Leeuw*, aan zyn regter poot door de verworpen en verbroken Thée-Pot der Amerikanen vermiakt, schynt al brullende zyn smart te klagen door 't openen van een muil, in welken hem zyne kiezen en een gedeelte zyner tanden schynen te ontbreeken.

3. De *Steendog* op 't ontwaaken van den Leeuw tot voor den Engelschman genaderd, staat met de staart tusschen de beenen den Leeuw aantekyken.

4. Een *uitgeputte Geldkist*, waar in de Rotten en Muizen aan de leedige geldzakken en gestempelde papieren knagen.

5. De *Koe* zeer vermagerd en buiten staat om langer melk te geven, zoekt voor haar hongerige maag voedzel aan doornen en distelen

6. De *Spanjaard*, met zyn aandeel van de gemolken melk te vreden, rust met zyn arm op den degen, die op de kolom zyner Amerikaansche staaten ligt.

7. De *Hollandsche Boer*, zeer in zyn schik met een vollen emmer melk, en, op zyn manier, met een mes gewapend, word in 't naar huis gaan tegengehouden door den Franschman, die

hem wyst naar het geene aan de overzyde van 't water geschied, doch waar aan de Hollander zich weinig schynt te stooren.

8. Aan de overzyde van 't water komen de *Commissarissen* by het Congress aan, dat verbeeld word onder de gedaante van eenen zittende Amerikaan omringt van twaalf andere personen. Het Congress wyst de Commissarissen op den Hoed van vryheid en heeft voor deszelfs voeten een verbroken Juk en gebroken Kluisters leggen. Aan de zyde van 't Congress staan Gerechtigheid, Wysheid, Sterkte en Voorzichtigheid, die met een straal van Hemel-licht beschenen worden, terwyl een andere Amerikaan zich bezig houdt met Goederen naar verschillende Oorden in te kuipen.

9. In 't verschiet ziet men het *Schip de Arend* in eenen slegten staat leggen, de Vlag halver stok wayende.

10. Voorts een gedeelte van een Vloot voerende *drie Leijen* in haare Vlag, van welke Vloot de Boot te rug komt, die met een Kyker was afgezonden om te zien hoe de Commissarissen zouden ontvangen worden, ten einde zich daar naar te regelen.

74. *THE BALLANCE OF POWER*

MAKER: R. S. (monogram)
PUBLISHER: Robert Wilkinson
DATE: January 17, 1781
SIZE: 9½" x 13¾" (24.1 cm. x 34.9 cm.)

NEW alliances among Continental nations were formed as the Revolution continued, and again the scale has been used to symbolize the shifting balance of power. Holding her shield and sword of justice and firmly outweighing the others, Britannia announces that "No one injures me with impunity." Her enemies struggle with little success to return the balance to their side. In despair, Indian Princess America fears that recent British victories will cause her defeat. Encouraged by France, Holland, losing coins from his pocket, attempts unsuccessfully to climb on the scale. He vows that he will do anything for money. Spain laments that much of her fleet has been lost to the British. A verse is placed at the bottom:

America, dup'd by a treacherous train,
Now finds she's a Tool both to France and to Spain;

Yet all three united can't weigh down the Scale:
So the *Dutchman* jumps in with the hope to prevail.
Yet *Britain* will boldly their efforts withstand,
And bravely defy them by Sea and by Land:
The *Frenchman* She'll Drub, and the *Spaniard*
She'll Beat
While the *Dutchman* She'll Ruin by Seizing his
Fleet:
Th' *Americans* too will with *Britons* Unite,
And each to the other be Mutual Delight.

This optimistic prediction of British victory was to be short-lived, as the battle of Yorktown effectively ended the Revolutionary War a few months later.

B.M. 5827   1960-93

160

The Ballance of Power

America, dup'd by a treacherous train,
Now finds she's a Tool both to France and to Spain;
Yet all three united   cant weigh down the Scale,
So the Dutchman jumps in with the hope to prevail.

The Ballance of Power
Yet Britain will boldly their efforts withstand,
And bravely defy them by Sea and by Land:

The Frenchman Shell Drub, and the Spaniard Shell Be
While the Dutchman Shell Ruin by Seizing his Fleet
Th' Americans too will with Britons Unite,
And each to the other be Mutual Delight.

London, Published as the Act directs, Jan.ʳ 17 1781 by R. Wilkinson, at N.º 58 in Cornhill.

75. *THE STATE NURSES.*

PUBLISHER: [Thomas Colley]
DATE: [October 1, 1781]
SIZE: 7″ x 10½″ (17.8 cm. x 26.6 cm.)

SLEEPING peacefully in a cradle rocked by Mansfield and Sandwich, the state nurses, the British lion is tucked safely under a rose-and-thistle-embossed blanket, symbolic of the increased influence of Scottish leaders on the crown. The lion is oblivious to the dogs, England's enemies, who bark out their various demands. Spain claims Gibraltar, Minorca, and Florida; France wants Barbados, Jamaica, Jersey, and so on; America, a black dog befouling the Tea Act bill, demands independence and no taxation; Holland proclaims neutrality and free navigation. The nurses attempt to shoo the howling animals away.

To the left rear the 1780 battle in which England wrested control of Gibraltar from Spain occurs, while on the right George III hunts deer at Windsor Castle. The satirist emphasizes the king's lack of interest in government affairs, which is why England needs "nurses."

B.M. 5850   1960-94

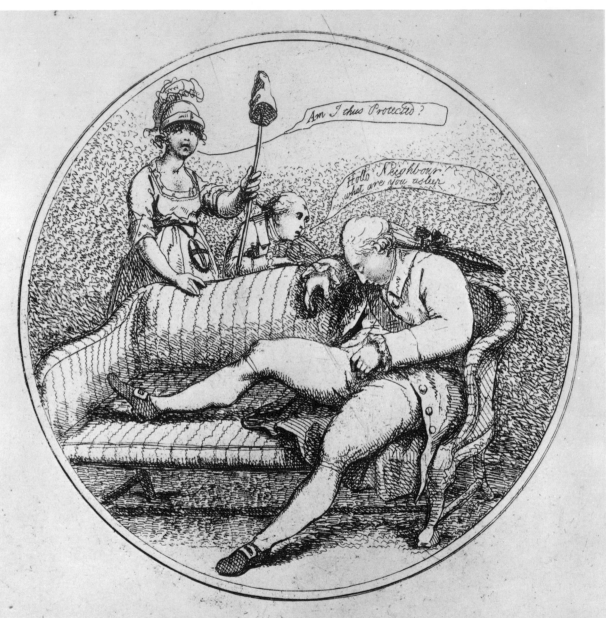

The State Watchman discover'd by the Genius of Britain,
studying plans for the Reduction of America.

Pub.d by T. Jones. 10. Dec. 1781.

76. *THE STATE WATCHMAN DISCOVER'D BY THE GENIUS OF BRITAIN*

MAKER: Attributed to Thomas Rowlandson
PUBLISHER: I. Jones
DATE: December 10, 1781
SIZE: 5½″ x 5¾″ (13.9 cm. x 14.6 cm.)

THOMAS ROWLANDSON is believed to have drawn this simple satire in which George III sleeps on the sofa, a pose often used to emphasize his apparent lack of concern about British policies.[1] Britannia, holding her liberty cap, complains, "Am I thus Protected?" A small man peers over the back of the sofa saying "Hollo Neighbour! what are you asleep?"

Published shortly after the British surrender at Yorktown, it expresses England's disappointment at the outcome of the war and America's surprise at the king's indifference.

B.M. 5856   1960-95

---

1. Joseph Grego in his two-volume work *Rowlandson the Caricaturist* (London, 1880) credits this satire to Rowlandson. This attribution continues in the British Museum catalog.

77. *THE ROYAL HUNT, OR A PROSPECT OF THE YEAR 1782.*

MAKER: South Briton
DESIGNER: North Briton (attributed to George Townshend)
PUBLISHER: R. Owen
DATE: February 16, 1782
SIZE: 10″ x 13¾″ (25.4 cm. x 34.9 cm.)

FOLLOWING the British defeat at Yorktown satirists turned their efforts to unseating the political leaders responsible for it and also suggested ways to restore England to a position of power. The international scope of Britain's problems continues to be symbolized by seashore settings, and numbered explanations are still present, although here only suggestive letters appear, leaving it up to the knowledgeable to fill in the blanks.

Attributed to George Townshend, by this time at the end of his career as a satirist, the print is a strong attack on Britain's politicians. A group of these men carouse in the left foreground, watched in disgust by the Opposition. Sitting between two loose women, (4) S---h (Sandwich) plays a violin and proclaims that now his only interest is in merry living. (5) N---h (North), seated on a bag inscribed Budg(et), yawns in boredom. (9) R---by (Richard Rigby), a former government supporter, has become critical and wishes Sandwich were in the bottomless pit (hell). (8) A---rst (Amherst) seeks Rigby's protection, and (7) G---mn (Lord George Germain) compares the situation to Minden, scene of his greatest military defeat in the French and Indian War.

For the Opposition (6) W--- P---t (William Pitt, the Younger) tells North to shake off his indolence; (3) F---x (Charles Fox) asks what happened to the navy and islands lost during the war; (2) B---k (Burke) questions why such disasters will not move leaders to action; and (1) R--- (duke of Richmond) curses the men made great by the ruin of their country.

On the right Britannia weeps as (10) "The Temple of Fame, formerly the Wonder of the World, but now in Ruins" is destroyed. Symbolic of England's crumbling empire, all but two columns have fallen. Holland, America, and France are pulling down Gibraltar, one of the two remaining, while the kings of France and Spain watch.

The temple is decorated with figures and inscriptions representing earlier successful English leaders and victories. A Scotsman tries to escape from a window, as blame for the disaster is placed on Bute and his faction.

Ships of the victorious nations approach the defeated British navy. The title derives from the final satiric touch, the royal hunt led by George III, a familiar comment on his disinterest in state affairs.

B.M. 5961   1960-97

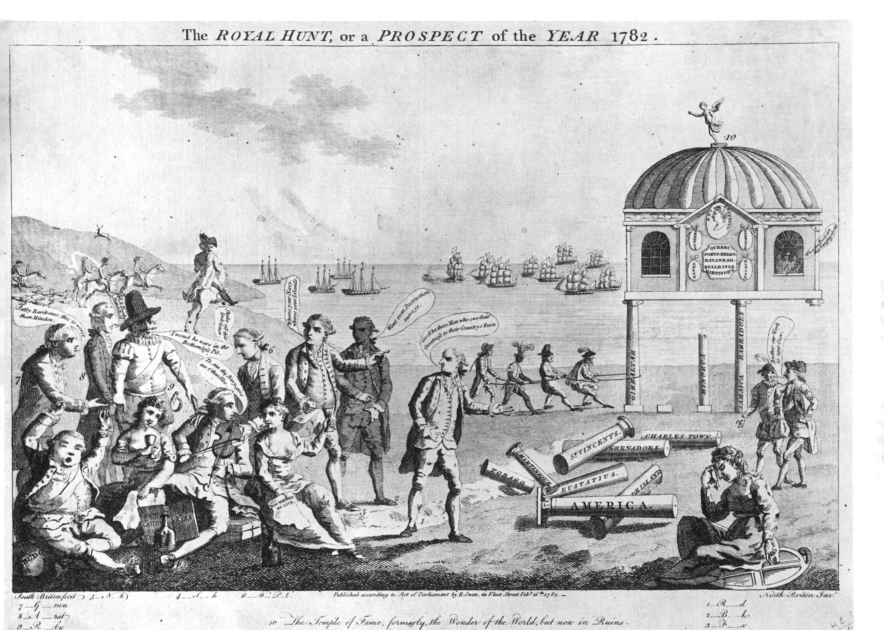

The ROYAL HUNT, or a PROSPECT of the YEAR 1782.

78. CHANGING PLACES; ALIAS FOX STINKING THE BADGER OUT OF HIS NEST.

MAKER: Attributed to James Gillray
PUBLISHER: [William Humphrey]
DATE: [March 22, 1782]
SIZE: 8″ x 11¾″ (20.3 cm. x 29.8 cm.)

AS anticipated, Lord North's ministry fell on March 20, 1782. Charles Fox became foreign secretary in the new government formed under Rockingham. Within two days, William Humphrey published this clever satire, which is firmly attributed to Gillray.[1] A badger, North, identified by his compass head, has emerged from a cave and is sent fleeing in the direction of Tower Hill by a fox (Charles Fox) who farts "eloquence" at him, a reference to his famous oratorical ability.[2]

On the ground near the animals are symbols of England's growing financial problems. A "Budget" bag containing soap and beer, referring to two of North's last unsuccessful tax proposals, lies open beside him. A sack, "Faro Bank," spills coins beneath Fox.[3] His personal monetary success after establishing a gaming house noted for that pastime raised hopes that Fox might conceive of a similar profitable scheme to rescue England from its fiscal problems.

Two other satiric representations add interest to the work. To the rear left stands a statue of "Janus," two-headed god of beginnings; one side shows a bearded old man (the defeated North) and the other a fox's head (Fox). At the rear right George III is hunting. However, he has been unseated over the last hurdle and is losing his crown, symbolic of the popular hope that he might be deposed.

B.M. 5964   1960-98

---

1. Mary Dorothy George changes a tentative attribution in the British Museum catalog to a more positive one in her book *English Political Caricature to 1792* (Oxford, 1959), p. 164.

2. Despite this reference, Lord North was never prosecuted for any state crime or sent to Tower Hill.

3. Faro was a popular eighteenth-century gambling card game.

Changing Places.—alias FOX stinking the (BADGER) out of his Nest.

79. *THE AMERICAN RATTLE SNAKE.*

MAKER: Attributed to James Gillray
PUBLISHER: William Humphrey
DATE: April 12, 1782
SIZE: 9⅞" x 14" (25.1 cm. x 35.5 cm.)

A SIMPLY designed satire, believed to be the work of Gillray, depicts the American rattlesnake, formerly shown disjointed as a symbol of the rebelling colonies, now whole and coiled into three sections. An exposed tongue is inscribed:

> Two British Armies I have thus Burgoyn'd,
> And room for more I've got behind.

British soldiers representing the surrendering forces of Burgoyne and Cornwallis are surrounded by two of the snake's circles. The remaining tail section is empty and advertises: "An Apartment to lett for Military Gentlemen." A verse beneath explains:

> Britons within the Yankeean Plains,
> Mind how ye March & Trench,
> The Serpent in the Congress reigns,
> As well as in the French.

B.M. 5973

1960-99

Britons within the Yankeean Plains,
Mind how ye March & Trench,

The AMERICAN RATTLE SNAKE.

Pub.d April 12.th 1782. by W.Humphrey, N.o 227 Strand.

The Serpent in the Congress reigns,
As well as in the French.

80. *THE POLITICAL MIRROR*

MAKERS: Razo Rezio, designer; Crunk Fogo, engraver
DATE: April 1782
SIZE: 6¼" x 9¼" (15.9 cm. x 23.5 cm.)

OBSERVED by new leaders and by Britannia, the defeated politicians tumble into an open pit presided over by the Devil. Britannia notes that had they remained in power they would have ruined her. Overhead Truth, an angel, reflects the political "Mirror of Truth" toward the pit.

The satirist provides each person with remarks appropriate to his present situation. Among the more familiar and influential ex-leaders are Bute, being carried through the air on the back of a witch labeled "England's Evil Genius"; Sandwich, still gripping a violin and requesting a whore and a bottle (see No. 77); and North, holding papers that represent his proposed taxes on soap, salt, and beer as he falls backward into the pit.

The new ministers, who were primarily pro-American during the Revolution, include Lord Camden, Edmund Burke, the duke of Richmond, and the current prime minister, the marquess of Rockingham. They pledge to return England to fiscal soundness and international power. From an otherwise black sky, rays of sun appear over the new ministers' heads to indicate that the new government would enjoy general approval.

B.M. 5982   1960-101

172

The POLITICAL MIRROR
or an EXHIBITION of MINISTERS for April 1782.

81. *BRITANIA'S ASSASSINATION.*

MAKER: Attributed to James Gillray
PUBLISHER: Elizabeth D'Archery
DATE: May 10, 1782
SIZE: 8⅝" x 13⅝" (21.9 cm. x 34.6 cm.)

THIS satire, attributed to James Gillray, is one of the boldest post-Revolutionary attacks leveled against the new ministry.[1] The blame for Britain's continued decline is squarely placed on the government, and the ministers are compared to its foreign enemies. In previous prints Britannia, in various allegorical guises, has been depicted undergoing dismemberment. Here she is again under attack. A fox (Charles Fox) bites at her remaining leg as Wilkes prepares to strike her with a document inscribed "Libel" and the duke of Richmond attacks with a musket. Now a government leader, Keppel, who was court-martialed and acquitted for inaction at the battle of Ushant in 1778, pulls down the British flag saying:

> "He that Fights & runs away,
> May live to fight another day."

Although the war had been over for several months when the satire was made, a peace treaty had not been concluded and foreign countries were still being blamed for England's defeat. An American Indian, holding Britannia's head in one hand and her arm with an olive branch in the other, runs away pursued by France, who hopes to forestall a separate peace agreement. Spain carries off Britannia's leg, Holland her shield.

The only defenders of the government are Edward Thurlow and Lord Mansfield, who have attached a rope to the statue and attempt to support it. In earlier works Mansfield, as a member of the former ministry, had often come under attack. Now he is depicted as one of the few remaining protectors of Britannia's rights.

B.M. 5987   1960-102

---

1. The attribution of this work to James Gillray was made by Mrs. George in the British Museum entry. The fact that in 1782 Gillray was employed by Elizabeth D'Archery, about whom little is known, is substantiated by Draper Hill, *Mr. Gillray The Caricaturist* (Greenwich, Conn., 1965), p. 23.

BRITANIA'S ASSASSINATION.

or ——— The Republicans Amusement.

82. *ANTICIPATION; OR, THE CONTRAST TO THE ROYAL HUNT.*

MAKER: Britons (attributed to Viscount Townshend)
PUBLISHER: William Wells
DATE: May 16, 1782
SIZE: 8½″ x 13½″ (21.6 cm. x 34.3 cm.)

THE ROYAL HUNT (No. 77), published only a few months after the surrender at Yorktown, was totally pessimistic about British affairs following the Revolution, but a more optimistic satire, similar in style and theme, appeared within a few months. The probable designer of both, Townshend, displays more confidence in the new ministry and depicts the rebuilding of England's temple of fame. The numbered figures are again identified by only the key letters of the person's name.

At the lower right Britannia holds an olive branch as she watches her temple being repaired. Although still supported by only two columns, they appear stronger, and previous enemy attempts to dislodge Gibraltar have been abandoned. The fallen column America is held upright by (1) C--n--y (Henry Conway), a government leader and colonial supporter throughout the conflict.

The upper part of the temple has been repaired. Figures of (2) F-x (Fox), (3) B---ke (Burke), and (4) C-md-n (Camden) appear at the right window to proclaim in Latin and English their interest in peace. From the left window (9) C-rlt-n (Carleton), the new commander in chief of the British forces, shoots the cock (Spain) that is about to fall on the head of a fleeing

Frenchman. New plaques representing naval leaders adorn the temple. To the rear Britain's rejuvenated fleet is battling an enemy.

In the center (5) S---h (Sandwich), a former minister, appears as a balladeer, a familiar reference to his interest in wine, women, and song. Lord North, in the left foreground, is now a stout washerwoman, a reminder that one of his last government acts had been to tax soap in order to bolster the British economy. George III undergoes an eye examination by Lord Rockingham, an oculist, who explains:

> --to nobler sights
> --the film removd
> which that false Gold that promisd
> clearer sight had bred.

In the distance (6) H---d (Hertford) laments his removal from government office while (7) S-ck--lle, the newly titled Germain, seeks a safe shelter.

In the left background an open building labeled "Tatershalls" depicts an auction of horses and hounds. George III's "Royal Hunt," the subject of several previous satires, has ended and he must now concentrate on affairs of state.

B.M. 5988

1958-415
Provenance: The Old Print Shop

The Prospect of the glorious restoration of the Temple of Fame.

ANTICIPATION; or, the CONTRAST to the ROYAL HUNT.

Publish'd May 16. 1782 by Wm Wells No 132 (opposite Salisbury Court) Fleet Street. London

1. C—n—y
2. F—x
3. B—ke
4. C—md—n
5. S——h
6. H——d
7. S—ck—lle
8. N—th
9. C—rlt—n

83. *THE RECONCILIATION BETWEEN BRITANIA AND HER DAUGHTER AMERICA.*

MAKER: Attributed to Thomas Colley
PUBLISHER: William Humphrey
DATE: About 1782
SIZE: 9¾" x 13¾" (24.7 cm. x 34.9 cm.)

THE scene of the reconciliation between Britain and America that appears as the cover of this volume was only one of a number of satires designed to comment on new national alliances at the close of the Revolution. Shortly after the cessation of fighting the British government began negotiations with representatives of the Continental Congress to arrange for a peace treaty separate from that of America's allies. France was particularly disturbed by this move, having expected, under the terms of a joint agreement, to make certain territorial gains at America's expense.

Britannia, sword and shield upright, and Indian Princess America with a liberty cap share the center of the work. Britannia says to America, "Be a good Girl and give me a Buss," and is answered, "Dear Mama say no more about it." America's wartime allies, displeased by her ready forgiveness of England, attempt to restrain her. France pulls on the ribbon linking America with himself and Spain, telling the latter, "Begar they will be friends again if you dont pull a little harder Cus. . . ." Spain replies, "Monsier Toad stool me do all I can to keep them asunder pull her hair, but take care she don't kick you." On the extreme left Holland, smoking a pipe and with a bottle of gin at his side, leans on a barrel of herrings and responds to unseen Catherine the Great's offer to mediate a settlement, "I'll Delliberate a little, to see which is weakest then I'll give you a direct answer Kate Rusia."

Gambling symbols at his feet, Fox is represented by a fox tail and head that says, "Sharp as a Sword." Fox himself comments, "Da-n that Frenchman & his Cousin Don, how they strain to part them. make haste my boy Keppel & give them a Spank." (See No. 81 for Keppel's new role in the ministry.) Keppel, barely visible at the right, replies, "that I will my Prince of bold Action they shall have fore and aft." The verse below explains:

1
A curse upon all Artifice
May Britons never thrive

2
While Roguish Minis—rs they keep
to Eat them up alive

3
By Lots they sell oh Dam—em Well
Each place we put our trust in.

4
Cut them of short twill make good sport
Whilst honest men are thrust in.

B.M. 5989   1960-158

The RECONCILIATION between BRITANIA and her daughter AMERICA,

1
A curse upon all Artifice
May Britons never thrive

2
While Roguish Minis-rs they keep
to Eat them up alive

3
By Lots they Sell oh Dam-em Well
Each place we put our trust in.

4
Cut them of short twill mak good sport
Whilst honest men are thrust in.

84. *THE BRITISH LION ENGAGING FOUR POWERS*

PUBLISHER: J. Barrow; SELLER: Richardson
DATE: June 14, 1782
SIZE: 14½″ X 9¾″ (36.8 cm. x 24.7 cm.)

AT the conclusion of the Revolution the nations of Europe struggled to extend their influence and authority in the world. It was therefore crucial for each of the participating countries to achieve the most satisfactory agreement possible during peace negotiations. To depict this continued aggressive spirit among the nations, satirists resorted to the symbolic use of animals. (See No. 2, the Aix-la-Chapelle *Congress of Brutes.)*

The scene has been changed from a conference table to an open field. With paw raised and tail held high the British lion tells the four allies, "You shall all have an old English drubbing to make you quiet." From the lower right corner a fox (Charles Fox) supports the lion, "I counsel your Majesty to give Monsieur the first gripe." A pug dog, Holland, responds, "I will be Jack of all sides as I have always been"; the snake, America, says, "I will have America and be Independent"; France, a cock, boasts, "I will have my Title from you and be call'd King of France"; and Spain, a dog, replies, "I will have Gibralter, that I may be King of all Spain." The verse below further explains the allusions:

> Behold the Dutch and Spanish Currs,
> Perfidious Gallus in his Spurs,
> And Rattlesnake with head upright
> The British Lion join to fight;
> He scorns the Bark, the Hiss, the Crow,
> That he's a Lion soon they'll know.

B.M. 6004   1960-103

The BRITISH LION engaging FOUR POWERS.

Pub.d by J. Barrow June 14: 1782. Sold by Richardson Print Seller, N. 68 High Holborn.

Behold the Dutch and Spanish Currs,
Perfidious Gallus in his Spurs,
And Rattlesnake with head upright,
The British Lion join to fight,
He scorns the Bark, the Hiss, the Crow,
That he's a Lion soon they'll know.

The WHIRLIGIG.
Alamode Beef, hot every Night.

The THUNDERER.

Vide; Every Man in his Humour, alterd from Ben Johnson.

85. *THE THUNDERER.*

MAKER: Attributed to James Gillray
PUBLISHER: Elizabeth D'Archery
DATE: August 20, 1782
SIZE: 13¼" x 9½" (33.6 cm. x 24.1 cm.)

AFTER distinguishing himself in the southern campaigns during the Revolution, Col. Banastre Tarleton returned to London a hero. This image was quickly tarnished as he adopted a flamboyant life style that included taking Mrs. Perdita Robinson as his mistress after she was abandoned by the prince of Wales. The satirists lost no time in making Tarleton an object of ridicule and scorn. In a work attributed to Gillray, Tarleton is depicted in a pose modeled after the famous portrait of him by Sir Joshua Reynolds, but he is presented as Bobadill, a vain, boastful character in Ben Jonson's play *Every Man in his own Humor*.[1] In bragging words he addresses the prince of Wales, who has only plumes for a head: "They have assaulted me some Three, Four, Five, Six of them together, & I have driven them afore me like a Flock of Sheep; . . ." Tarleton continues to enumerate his con-

quests. The prince responds, "I'd as lief as twenty Crowns I could Talk as fine as you, Capt."

The maker has set the satire before a brothel, symbolized most prominently by the figure of a whore, legs outstretched, and further identified, "This is the Lad'll Kiss most sweet. Who'd not love a Soldier?" The vine branch stuck in the sign indicates that wine is also available.

Below the title is added "Vide: Every Man in his Humour, alter'd from Ben Johnson."

B.M. 6116   1960-105

---

1. Jonson's play, first performed in London in 1598, was revived in 1751 by David Garrick, the famous actor, and became a standard repertory piece during the rest of the century.

86. *THE HABEAS CORPUS, OR THE WILD GEESE FLYING AWAY WITH FOX TO AMERICA.*

PUBLISHER: F. Barrow
DATE: August 27, 1782
SIZE: 9¼″ x 13½″ (23.5 cm. x 34.3 cm.)

BIRDS, though less frequently employed as symbolic references in eighteenth-century satires, are here effectively used to present British leaders' views concerning peace negotiations at the close of the Revolution, along with the part Charles Fox was playing.

Just before this print was made, Fox had shared the position of secretary of state with William Shelburne. The two found themselves differing on the manner in which the agreement should be pursued, Shelburne favoring joint negotiations with America and France, and Fox advocating a separate treaty granting America immediate independence. When Shelburne became prime minister upon Lord Rockingham's sudden death in July 1782, Fox resigned his post.

Public opinion was fairly divided on the question; the designer of this print presents an anti-Fox viewpoint. A flock of wild geese connected by a ribbon, one end of which is attached to the rear leg of a fox, prepares to fly him over the ocean. Fox says, "I hope they will bear me safe to the dear Independent Congress." The birds represent those factions in English political life that wished him out of government affairs. Their position is best summed up by one of the geese who comments, "He is fitter to sit in Congress than in a British Parliament."

B.M. 6029   1960-104

184

The Habeas Corpus, or The Wild Geese flying away with Fox to America.

87. *WONDERS WONDERS WONDERS & WONDERS*

PUBLISHER: I. Langham
DATE: November 9, 1782
SIZE: 10⅓" x 15¼" (26.2 cm. x 38.7 cm.)

CONTINUING the comment on the shifts of political and national alliances following the Revolution, this satire focuses on the new friendships of former enemies. The Colonial Williamsburg impression was published in 1782 by John Lanham and contains none of the dialogue included in the copy at the British Museum, which was sold by William Humphrey in 1783.

Dominating the center are the English ministers: Fox, with appropriate head, Shelburne to the left, and Lord Denbigh with the body of a foxhound. The conversation in the later edition explains: Fox, "I now will play the Foxes Part, And gain a Secret from each Heart"; Shelburne, "I should not have used you so ill, If I had not swallow'd a Scotch Pill"; Denbigh, "Through you & Burke I lost my Place, Yet I forgive the sad Disgrace."

On the left Britannia with shield and sword upright and Indian Princess America with staff and liberty cap shake hands and vow friendship. In a similar pose on the right Wilkes addresses George III, "Your M . . . . . y (Majesty) has been long deceiv'd, And at your Subjects was much griev'd." The king responds, "Enough! my Fault I own, my Subject Loyal, And you much love, 'pon my Word Royal."

At the left rear the duke of Richmond joins hands with cleric Henry Bate, a strong antigovernment critic, and to the right Sir Hugh Palliser and Keppel, both naval leaders pledge to forget their previous bitter disputes.

Beneath the print is a verse:

If Kat----to can Bring Such Wonders to pass
He sure deserves the Honor to Kiss the Kings ---

Kat---to (Katerfelto) was a notorious quack of the period who claimed to be able to bring about miracles. The satirist suggests that these friendships are in the nature of his marvels. Since attempts at reconciliation were politically motivated, the "wonder" would last only a short time.

B.M. 6162   1960-106

186

WONDERS WONDERS WONDERS &

DEDICATED *to the Wonderfull* WONDERS *Wonderfull Wonderer*

Publish'd as the Act Directs Nov. 9 1782 By I Langham PRINT

If Kat——to can Bring Such Wonders to pass
He sure deserves the Honor to Kiss the Kings

Coulerer N⁰ 34 Dorset Street Salisbury Court Fleet Street

88. *THE HORRORS OF WAR A VISION OR A SCENE IN THE TRAGEDY OF RICHD: 3.*

PUBLISHER: Daniel Wilson
DATE: December 1, 1782
SIZE: 9½″ x 13⅛″ (24.1 cm. x 33.3 cm.)

FIRST published in August 1782 by John Sharpe, this satire was copied in December by Daniel Wilson, whose work is shown here. Almost timeless in its implications, the horrors of war—in this instance, the American Revolution—are brought home to the defeated English ministers.

To the right an unidentified leader, possibly Sandwich, with a look of horror on his face, watches from his couch as the drama unfolds. On the left, Lord North watches and comments, "Perdition seize thee! Had'st thou finished the intended Purpose, the triumphs of the junto had been complete. But now disgrace and public detestation, mark the awful resignation of our Places." A satyrlike figure of a woman, Corruption, holds out a cup to a seated Britannia saying, "My good lord, I have nearly done her business." Britannia responds, "Oh I have drank of the deadly pois'ned cup adminst'red by corruption." The Indian Princess America stands on a cloud that covers four naked, dead children and some weapons of war. She addresses the prone leader, "Can'st thou behold this mangled beast—this dreadful carnage of my children & feel no keen remorse! Oh forego this bloody warfare, else can revolted nature 'eer forget her wrongs or close

in amity the dire catastrophe of recent woes." He replies, "Hence bloody Phantom! Shake not thy gory locks at me. Approach thou like the rugg'd Rhinoceros, or fierce Hyrcanian beast take any shape but that, & my firm nerves shall never tremble." Behind him yet another deposed leader examines a map of the British Empire in 1775 and comments: "O'er America's lofty summits And Africa's dusky plains: From Europe to the Ganges: And wher'eer the Atlantic bathes the western shores," an accurate description of Britain's pre-Revolutionary empire.

The title satirically suggests that the actions of English politicians which precipitated the Revolution and cost their country so many lost lives and territories were not unlike those perpetrated with equally disastrous results by Richard III and his supporters.[1]

B.M. 6024   1960-107

---

1. Following David Garrick's successful 1743 appearance on the London stage in Shakespeare's *Richard III,* Hogarth painted and then engraved his portrait in the role. It certainly must have served as the inspiration for this satire by an unknown maker.

The HORRORS of WAR a VISION Or a Scene in the Tragedy of Rich.ᵈ 3.

London, Published as the Act directs, Dec.ᵗ 1ˢᵗ 1782, by D. Wilson.

89. *THE BELLIGERANT PLENIPO'S*

MAKER: Thomas Colley
PUBLISHER: W. Richardson
DATE: December 6, 1782
SIZE: 9¾" x 13¾" (24.7 cm. x 34.9 cm.)

SATIRIC depictions of the peace negotiations following the Revolution continue as five plenipotentiaries, each holding his country's flag, represent the five powers involved in the conflict. Each stands on a separate island symbolic of the individual positions maintained by their respective countries during the talks.

Wearing only half a crown, George III stands on the left before an empty purse, an arm, and a foot, saying, "I give them Independance." France, his severed arm at Britain's feet, declares, "I must have Canada an Grenada for my Arm." Holland is a weeping figure on crutches; his amputated foot before George symbolizes financial losses during the war. He insists on Eustatia and Ceylon in retribution. Forced to wear a peg leg, Spain demands Gibraltar for his injury. Last comes a scantily clad, smiling Indian Princess America who holds the other half of George's crown and the liberty cap. She proclaims: "I have got all I wanted Empire!" Above, half-shrouded in clouds, appears Hibernia (Ireland) announcing that "I deny all foreign Jurisdictions & will roast my own potatoes." This refers to Ireland's desire to follow America's example and achieve independence from Britain.

Preliminary articles of peace had been signed only days before this satire was published, and it is clear that the designer was not fully aware of all of their terms. France did not negotiate for Canada and had already recaptured Eustatia, thereby disregarding Holland's claims, while America's recognition as an independent nation still depended on an agreement between Great Britain and France.

The Colonial Williamsburg impression of the print differs slightly from the copy in the British Museum, which is not dated and indicates that it was sold by W. Humphrey, who may simply have become Richardson's agent.

B.M. 6051 altered

1972-82
PROVENANCE: The Old Print Shop

The BELLIGERANT PLENIPO'S

AMERICA TRIUMPHANT and BRITANNIA in DISTRESS

EXPLANATION.

I America sitting on that quarter of the globe with the Flag of the United States displayed over her head, holding in one hand the Olive branch, inviting the ships of all nations to partake of her commerce; and in the other hand supporting the Cap of Liberty.

II Fame proclaiming the joyful news to all the world.

III Britannia weeping at the loss of the trade of America, attended with an evil genius.

IV The British flag struck, on her strong Fortresses.

V French, Spanish, Dutch, &c. shipping in the harbours of America.

VI A view of New-York, wherein is exhibited the Trator Arnold, taken with remorse for selling his country, and Judas like hanging himself.

90. *AMERICA TRIUMPHANT AND BRITANNIA IN DIS'TRESS'*

PLACE OF PUBLICATION: [America]
PUBLISHER: [Weatherwise's *Town & Country Almanac*]
DATE: [1782]
SIZE: 6½" x 7¼" (16.5 cm. x 18.4 cm.)

MANY of the satires in this volume comment on America's victory over Britain in the Revolutionary War, but none is of more importance than the work shown here because it was one of only a few that appeared in an American publication. Not only does the designer celebrate the triumph of America, but more important he depicts the overtures of reconciliation and friendship tendered by the colonies to the defeated mother country. The figures are numbered and a full explanation appears at the bottom: I. "America sitting on that quarter of the globe with the Flag of the United States displayed over her head; holding in one hand the Olive branch, inviting the ships of all nations to partake of her commerce; and in the other hand [a staff] supporting the Cap of Liberty." II. "Fame proclaiming the joyful news to all the world." III. "Britannia weeping at the loss of the trade of America, attended with an evil genius." IV. "The British flag struck, on her strong Fortresses." V. "French, Spanish, Dutch, &c. shipping in the harbours of America." VI. "A view of New=York, wherein is exhibited the Trator [Benedict] Arnold, taken with remorse for selling his country, and Judas like hanging himself."

B.M. Not listed   1960-124

91. *BLESSED ARE THE PEACE MAKERS*

PUBLISHER: [Elizabeth D'Archery]
DATE: [February 24, 1783]
SIZE: 9½″ x 13½″ (24.1 cm. x 34.3 cm.)

IN the continuing commentary on the peace negotiations George III is led by his enemies down a country road toward a building labeled "Inquisition." The symbolic use of this term suggests that England will suffer for its position during the American Revolution. Spain, usually depicted as a don but now attired in a more conventional coat and breeches, leads the march. Next comes France, who holds one end of a rope that is tied around George's neck. The king walks between two vertical spears with a third acting as a crossbar on which the English royal emblems—lion, crown, and unicorn—are precariously balanced. Shelburne follows, carrying a document inscribed "Preliminaries," representing the initial peace agreement. America, a slim man wearing a tightly buttoned waistcoat and breeches, is next. He flails the air with a whip inscribed "America" which, if brought down, threatens to strike both Shelburne and the king. America has tied a rope around the neck of Holland, who, hands in pockets, seems reluctant to participate in the punishment, a reflection of the true state of affairs because that nation was almost totally neglected during the negotiations.

B.M. 6174   1960-108

Blessed are the PEACE MAKERS

92. *BOREAS HELPING THE PATRIOTIC WEATHER-COCK TO SNAP A GOOSE.*

PUBLISHER: J. Barrow
DATE: April 4, 1783
SIZE: 14″ x 9½″ (35.6 cm. x 24.1 cm.)

EARLY in 1783 a strange alliance of two former enemies occurred. In a last-ditch effort to regain some of his lost power, Fox agreed to join North, a man he had long condemned, in attempting to unseat Shelburne, the prime minister. In 1782 J. Barrow, reflecting public opinion, had published the anti-Fox satire (No. 86) that commented on his break with government policy during the peace negotiations by depicting a flock of geese flying Fox to America. Now Fox was back in favor, and Barrow published this sequel to the affair less than two months later.

Lord North, his head just barely visible to the left, appears as Boreas, symbol of the North Wind, blowing the geese that would have flown him away toward Fox, a weathervane. The weathervane symbolism for Fox sug-gests his proclivity to alter his opinions on important issues to conform to public sentiment. Representing his political enemies, the geese are threatened by Fox's open mouth. The verse accompanying the print describes the scene:

> MARS doth his Iron Chariot stop,
> And it's a General Peace:
> Boreas with Fox hath made it up,
> And freely blows him Geese.
>
> A Weather-cock to snap a Goose,
> May seem a Paradox;
> The Policy needs no Excuse;
> The Weather-cock's a Fox.

B.M. Not listed

1957-62
PROVENANCE: The Old Print Shop

Boreas helping the patriotic Weather-cock to snap a Goose.

MARS doth his Iron Chariot stop,
And it's a General Peace:
Boreas with Fox hath made it up,
And freely blows him Geese.

A Weather-cock to snap a Goose,
May seem a Paradox;
The Policy needs no Excuse;
The Weather-cock's a Fox.

Pub.d by J. Barrow. April 4.d 1783. White Lion Bull Stairs Surryside Black Friars Bridge.

93. *THE TIMES, ANNO 1783.*

MAKER: Attributed to James Gillray
PUBLISHER: William Humphrey
DATE: April 1, 1783
SIZE: 9¼" x 14½" (23.5 cm. x 36.8 cm.)

NO lasting peace followed the Revolution either in England or on the Continent, for one dispute succeeded another. A work attributed to Gillray comments on them. Upper right a demon powered by excreted gas "Poor John Bull! Ha! Ha! Ha!" flies off toward America with a map of the new nation. Stout John Bull, England, laments, " 'Tis lost! Irrecoverably lost!", a reference to American independence. France consoles Bull with a pinch of snuff saying, "Ah. Ah. Me Lord Angla, volez vous une pince de Snuff, for de Diable will not give you back de Amerique." Attired as a Don, an incensed Spain comments, "See Gibralter! See Don Langara! by St. Anthony you have made me the Laughing Stock of Europe." Holland, wearing a flowerpot hat, laments, "De Donder take you Monseuir, I think I have paid the Piper."

The strategically located fort of Gibralter had been the object of much dispute during the Revolution, and Spain was induced to enter the war by French promises of aid in regaining it. When the preliminary peace agreement was formalized on February 6, 1783, however, the struggle ended with England firmly in control. The battle scene in the background suggests that the possession of Gibraltar would continue to be a controversial subject.

B.M. 6210   1960-110

The TIMES, Anno. 1783.

Pub.d Apr.l 14.th 1783 by W. Humphrey, N.o 227 Strand.

94. *AMUSEMENT FOR JOHN BULL & HIS COUSIN PADDY, OR, THE GAMBOLS OF THE AMERICAN BUFFALO, IN ST. JAMES'S STREET.*

PUBLISHER: John Fielding
DATE: May 1, 1783
SIZE: 3½″ x 5¹⁵/₁₆″ (8.9 cm. x 15.1 cm.)

THIS amusing and somewhat unusual satire was designed for one of London's newer publications, the *European Magazine*. It comments on certain similarities in the American and Irish rebellions which in 1783 were being resolved. England did not have sufficient troops to suppress the conflicts in both countries, so those in Ireland were withdrawn and sent to America. Local Irish forces were then organized, but they would pledge allegiance only to George III and not to the government leaders. In 1783 the British government agreed to loosen its hold on Ireland and grant it more freedom to act in its own right, just as it was forced to do by the American colonies. The maker has been far less precise in individual characterizations in this print than was usual for the period, but the message conveyed is unmistakable.

The American buffalo has charged through St. James's Street, throwing vendor and wares to the ground.[1] Leaders of the newly formed coalition government are left in a turmoil as they fight to retrieve the scattered loaves and fishes symbolizing new government policies no more popular with the Americans and Irish than previous ones. Although restrained by Edward Thurlow, a judge forced out of office by Fox but now obviously courting favor, the buffalo appears ready to charge again. George III, an expression of amusement on his face, watches the scene from a window overhead.

In a departure from the usual structure of satires, one of the main figures, Ireland, is not actually depicted. As the title suggests, however, Cousin Paddy should share John Bull's amusement in seeing policies destructive to the nation's well being overthrown.

B.M. 6223   1960-112

1. This is one of the earliest symbolic representations of America as a buffalo. Whether Fielding had any personal knowledge of it as a native American species or simply based his idea on an European concept of the animal's potential strength cannot be determined. It makes an ideal foil for the symbolizing of Britain as a bull, because a buffalo suggests a slightly more powerful animal—a necessary representation of America at the close of the Revolution.

95. *REBUS: THE(ASS)-HEADED AND (COW-HEART)-ED MINISTRY MAKING THE BRITISH (LION) GIVE UP THE PULL*

PUBLISHER: J. Barrow
DATE: May 8, 1783
SIZE: 8¹¹/₁₆″ x 15¾″ (22.1 cm. x 40 cm.)

ANIMALS are effectively substituted for words in the rebus-like title and are also employed in the satire to represent the nations striving to reach a satisfactory peace treaty following the Revolution. A great harness with the British lion on one side and the four allied nations on the other is joined over the center of a pit and each side strives to pull the other into the hole. A rope attached to the lion's head is held by ass-headed ministers whose comments display their lack of agreement on terms for the treaty. As the title suggests, this may contribute to the lack of force (pull) of the British lion.

The enemies—Spain, now a hound, the French cock, the American rattlesnake, and pug dog Holland—are concerned that the proposed treaty might be more favorable to the British if only its leaders could agree among themselves. Above, a double-headed eagle, Russia, straddles the pit to symbolize its continued neutral stance.

The lion's lengthy verse states the problem clearly:

> My honour'd Sirs, who me pretend to lead,
> Tis plain the office does not sute your head.
> Your hearts like mine all dangers should engage,
> The more my foes, the more enflam'd I rage.
> Who leads a Lion, should himself be bold,
> But you are Dastards, and it shall be told.
> By France I'm injured, yet you ask them peace,
> What shall I call you? puppies, sheep, or geese?

> To know you're such, go ask each British Tar,
> Which would a Frenchman ask to end a war.
> O'er the Atlantic, in the martial field,
> You held me in, and now you make me yield;
> And tho' I'm able to maintain my State,
> I fall by Goose-caps, and by Fox's prate.
> I want the brave to lead me on to fight,
> To scorn a Peace, till I have all my right,
> But you're scarce fit to lead me out to sh----
> How hard my fate that such should me control,
> Who realy are without a British Soul,
> For ever blush, for all the wise can see,
> You are but Asses and make one of me.

The inscription below the title places the blame for Britain's condition:

> This Plate is designed for a Memorial of the Strength of the British Constitution, being able to cope with four Powers: and also to truly represent a Set of frantic, sophistical Patriots, who when they had wrangled themselves into Ministry, found themselves intirely incapable of the Task, Therefore very suddenly made very humiliating Concessions to France, to obtain a Peace, to the great Mortification of every true Briton, (the British Lion being in full strength and had just obtain'd some glorious victories over the French and Spaniards.) Thus by a desponding Ministry America got Independency, and France attain'd all her perfidious ends.

B.M. 6229   1960-113

202

ARCH. *and this Col. I am afraid has*   SCRUB & ARCHER   SCRUB *Converted; ay and perverted*
Converted the Affection of Your Perdita   *my Dear Friend; for I am Afraid he has Made*
her a Whore &c.

Pub. Aug. 1783 by W. Humphrey N227 Strand.

96. *SCRUB & ARCHER*

MAKER: J. B. (John Boyne)
PUBLISHER: William Humphrey
DATE: August 1, 1783
SIZE: 7⅜″ x 6⅞″ (18.7 cm. x 17.5 cm.)

WHILE most of the satires during and immediately following the Revolutionary War were directed toward international situations, works of a more personal nature were not neglected. Members of the new coalition government, many of whom had been political enemies only a short time before, were particularly vulnerable to pictorial ridicule. When these same leaders became involved in a growing number of romantic intrigues, the satirist did not have to search far to find new ideas for his work.

John Boyne found the inspiration for this print in the characters of George Farquhar's popular play, *The Beaux' Stratagem*, a comedy that deals with the fortunes of two friends, Scrub and Archer, and their escapades in love. The British Museum impression is dated April 1783 and has Boyne as the engraver and publisher, but by August, as recorded on the Colonial Williamsburg copy, Humphrey was acting in the latter capacity.

Fox, on the left in the guise of Scrub, and Lord North, on the right as Archer, two former political enemies, had united in a coalition government. Gipsy, a lady's maid, represents Mrs. Perdita Robinson, who obviously is attempting to overhear what the two men are saying. On the wall is a print of Colonel Tarleton (see No. 85), who vied with Fox for Mrs. Robinson's attentions. The conversation is a clever double entendre, because although it centers on the romantic entanglement, it also pokes fun at the new friendship:

ARCH: And this Col: I am Afraid has Converted the Affection of your Perdita

SCRUB: Converted; ay and perverted my Dear Friend for I am Afraid he has Made her a Whore &c.

B.M. 6221   1960-111

97. *ALL ALIVE OR THE POLITICAL CHURCHYARD.*

PUBLISHER: B. Pownall
DATE: August 9, 1783
SIZE: 8⅞" x 13¼" (22.5 cm. x 33.6 cm.)

THE tomb and graveyard symbolism periodically employed in satiric design is used here to comment effectively on the British political leaders involved in the Revolution and the subsequent peace negotiations. Each of the tombs and stones has appropriate markers; most are inscribed with only the key letters of the individual's name and caustic comments on his activities. Today a number of them are unknown or long forgotten and can be recognized only by students of British political history. But the principal government figures have appeared in many of the satires in this volume, and their markers are easily understood.

The three front center stones are reserved as follows: Burke, left, "Here Lieth Edd. B---e Oeconomist Extraordinary To his Majesty. To Save his breath He welcom'd death." North, center, "Here Lieth L--d N--H. I'm gone to realms below, To find more Cause for woe." Fox, right: "Here Lieth C---S F--X. The game I have play'd, I have lost by a Spade, My partner was wrong For he shuffl'd to long."

An elaborately decorated pyramid tomb surrounded by a fence stands in the center. Belonging to Pitt, it is inscribed: "Here Lieth The Honble Wm P--tt. Thou cov'rest Earth Unequall'd Worth."

Just behind Burke's tomb to the left is that of King George: "I gover'nd all with --- decree But now alas, Death governs me." Placing his tomb to the rear of his ministers' again emphasizes the subordinate position he assumed during the war.

As suggested by the title, all of the politicians are alive, but their political careers are either completely over or are in danger. The king, of course, would continue to reign for many years, but always under the influence of others.

B.M. 6256   1960-114

All ALIVE or The POLITICAL CHURCH YARD.

98. *DOMINION OF THE SEAS.*

PUBLISHER: Elizabeth D'Archery
DATE: December 1, 1783
SIZE: 8½″ x 11½″ (21.6 cm. x 29.2 cm.)

BY late 1783 Britain had regained partial control of the seas, and this satire comments on the Revolutionary allies who must now respect its restored power. The satirist symbolizes Britannia in the recently preferred peace pose, with an olive branch in one hand and a staff supporting two British flags in the other. She sits in a small boat moored in waters, identified as Portland Road, accompanied only by a small weasel-like animal, intended to represent Fox, perched on the prow.[1] An approaching vessel carries the representatives of Holland, Spain, France, and America. Although each dips his country's flag into the water in a gesture of homage, their facial expressions belie any pleasure at the situation.

Below the picture is printed the following explanation: "BRITANNIA on board the FOX safe Moor'd in PORTLAND-road—As Mistress of the Sea, she receives Homage from the whole World. NB A distinction contended for by our present Peace Makers." The NB is a direct reference to the continuing dispute among the nations for control of the seaways.

B.M. 6274   1960-157

1. The duke of Portland, William Henry Cavendish, was prime minister briefly in the coalition government controlled by Fox and North.

Portland Road

DOMINION of the SEAS.

BRITANNIA *on board the* FOX *safe Moor'd in* PORTLAND-road ——— *As Mistress of the Sea, she receives Homage from the whole World.* NB *A distinction contended for by our present Peace Makers.*

Pub.d by E. Dachery St James's Street. Dec.r 1.st 1783.

THE HISTORICAL PAINTER.

99. *THE HISTORICAL PAINTER.*

MAKER: W. D. (William Dent)
PUBLISHER: J. Cattermoul
DATE: February 10, 1784
SIZE: 9¼″ x 9¼″ (23.5 cm. x 23.5 cm.)

ATTIRED in seventeenth-century dress symbolic of Cromwell, Fox, whose plumed hat proclaims him a man of moderation, is painting a picture of the execution of Charles I, using his scepter for a brush and the bottom of a crown for the palette. Justice, eyes fully open to Fox's political policies, stands with sword upraised ready to strike him from behind. In her other hand she holds a scale. A small fox sitting in one pan is outweighed by "Loyalty" in the other. A partly unsheathed sword inscribed "Commonwealth" and a book "Patriotism by C. Cromwell" lie on the floor by Fox. A cat crouches beside them. On the wall hangs a painting of a standing fox presenting an Indian, America, with a document labeled "Independence."

About 1780 satirists began to find that there was great similarity between the actions of Cromwell and Fox, and a number of makers, including the Dutch (No. 72), found it convenient to compare the two. Both were leaders of opposition movements who occasionally found themselves allied with former enemies, both were politically ambitious and would go to any length to achieve their aims. Cromwell brought about the downfall and execution of Charles I. This satire suggests that a politically ambitious Fox might resort to similar measures to gain his ends.

B.M. 6408   1960-115

100. *THE LOSS OF EDEN,!–AND EDEN,! LOST.*

MAKER: Attributed to Thomas Rowlandson
PUBLISHER: W. Hinton
DATE: December 21, 1785
SIZE: 9¾″ x 14″ (24.7 cm. x 35.6 cm.)

THE American Revolution continued to provide topical material for satires long after peace was declared. Since most of them were unsigned, only speculative attributions can be made. The style and technique of this are typical of Thomas Rowlandson.

Like a number of public officials portrayed in the last few satires, William Eden had a proclivity to alter his political thinking to correspond to popular opinion. Rowlandson comments on one such change that suggested similarities to Benedict Arnold's treasonous actions during the Revolution. This was not the first time that Eden had come under such satiric attack. (See Nos. 42 and 43.) Having held a number of official positions and having been highly successful in solving the Irish economic problems, Eden chose to leave the government, in opposition to many policies. When William Pitt, the Younger, needed a qualified minister to negotiate an important but highly controversial commercial treaty with France, he solicited Eden's aid. Eden's former associates immediately criticized his capitulation to the "enemy," and Rowlandson was provided with material for his satire.

Holding a pen in one hand and a paper inscribed "Liberty" in the other, Eden approaches Arnold, who, sword outstretched behind him, is saying "Liberty." From his coat Eden trails papers labeled "commissn to America; £6,000 pr Annum," and "Commercl Negotiator to France." The subtitle notes, "NB every Man has his Price Sr Robt Walpole's Politicks" and the verse beneath comments on the comparison of Eden with Arnold:

Two PATRIOTS (in the self same (Age was Born,)
And both alike have gain'd the Public scorn,
This to America did much pretend.
The other was to Ireland a Friend,
Yet SWORD or ORATORY, would not do,
As each had different Plans in Veiw,
AMERICA lost! ARNOLD & Alass!
To loose our EDEN now is come to pass.

B.M. 6815   1960-116

212

BIBLIOGRAPHY

The American Heritage Book of The Revolution. New York: American Heritage Publishing Co., 1958. Illus.

Atherton, Herbert M. *Political Prints in the Age of Hogarth: A Study of the Ideographic Representation of Politics.* Oxford: Clarendon Press, 1974. Illus.

Boatner, Mark Mayo, III. *Encyclopedia of the American Revolution.* New York: David McKay Company, Inc., 1966.

————. *Landmarks of the American Revolution.* Harrisburg, Pa.: Stackpole Books, 1973.

British Museum. Department of Prints and Drawings. *Catalogue of Prints and Drawings in the British Museum.* Division I. *Political and Personal Satires.* London: Printed by Order of the Trustees, 1870-1954. Vols. 1-4 prepared by Frederic George Stephens; Vols. 5-11 by Mary Dorothy George. Title changes with Vol. 5 to *Catalogue of Political and Personal Satires Preserved in the Department of Prints and Drawings in the British Museum.*

Colonial Society of Massachusetts. *Boston Prints and Printmakers, 1670-1775.* Boston, 1973. Illus.

George, M. Dorothy. *English Political Caricature: A Study of Opinion and Propaganda.* Vol. 1: *to 1792.* Vol. 2: *1793-1832.* Oxford: Clarendon Press, 1959. Illus.

Hill, Draper. *Mr. Gillray The Caricaturist: A Biography.* London: Phaidon Press Ltd., 1965. Illus.

Mayor, Alpheus Hyatt. *Prints and People: A Social History of Printed Pictures.* New York: Metropolitan Museum of Art, 1971. Illus.

Museum of Graphic Art. *American Printmaking, The First 150 Years.* Washington, D. C.: Smithsonian Institution Press, 1969.

National Portrait Gallery. *"The Dye Is Now Cast": The Road to American Independence, 1774-1776.* Washington, D. C.: Smithsonian Institution Press, 1975. Illus.

———. *In the Minds and Hearts of the People, Prologue to the American Revolution: 1760-1774.* Greenwich, Conn.: New York Graphic Society, 1974. Illus.

Paulson, Ronald, comp. *Hogarth's Graphic Works.* 2 vols. 2d rev. edn. New Haven: Yale University Press, 1970. Illus.

———. *Hogarth: His Life, Art, and Times.* 2 vols. New Haven: Yale University Press, 1971. Illus.

Riely, John C. *The Age of Horace Walpole in Caricature.* New Haven: Yale University Library, 1973. Illus.

Walpole Society. *Prints Pertaining to America.* Charlottesville: University Press of Virginia, 1963. Illus.

Wardroper, John. *Kings, Lords and Wicked Libellers: Satire and Protest, 1760-1837.* London: John Murray Ltd., 1973. Illus.

Winterthur Conference Report, 1970. *Prints in and of America to 1850,* John D. Morse, ed. Charlottesville: University Press of Virginia, 1970. Illus.

INDEX

Entries in boldface refer to illustration numbers.

Franklin, Benjamin, no. **11, 34** (untitled satire); also 6, 43
French and Indian War, 2, 3, 18, 20, 22, 28, 50, 126, 146, 166
Frontenac, 28

Gage, Gen. Thomas, 63
Garrick, David, 188
Gay, John, *The Beggar's Opera*, 9
Genoa: symbolized as dog, 16
George II, king of England, 18
George III, king of England, 45, 49, 52, 56, 89, 93, 112, 122, 130, 150, 152, 156, 162, 165, 166, 168, 176, 186, 190, 194, 200, 206
George, Mary Dorothy: *British Museum Catalogs*, 6, 11 n. 7, 101 n. 1, 174 n. 1; *English Political Caricature*, 10 n. 1, 11 n. 8, 27 n. 2, 36 n. 1, 38 n. 1, 168 n. 1
Germain, Lord George, 93, 124, 166, 176
Gibraltar, 16, 49, 136, 162, 166, 176, 180, 190, 198
Gillray, James, 118, 120, 130, 168, 170, 174, 183, 198
Glatz, 16
Gods: as symbols, 18, 20, 74, 150
Gordon, Lord George, 132, 150
Grafton, Augustus Henry Fitzroy, duke of, 38, 49, 52
Great Britain: symbolized as beast, half man–half vulture, 108; Britannia, 8, 15, 18, 20, 28, 43, 45, 58, 70, 74, 101, 106, 116, 130, 140, 160, 165, 166, 172, 174, 176, 178, 186, 188, 193, 208, 211; bull, 120, 122, 124; bust, 36; cow, 94, 158; dog, 140, 146; John Bull, 9, 118, 198; leopard, 145; lion, 9, 16, 18, 20, 22, 94, 106, 126, 130, 154, 158, 162, 180, 194, 202; male, 90, 138, 142, 148, 154; sailor, 18, 20; wheels, 52
Greenwich Hospital, 115
Grego, Joseph, *Rowlandson the Caricaturist*, 165 n. 1
Grenada, 11 n. 4, 145, 190
Grenville, George, 3, 36, 38

Guttenberg, Carl, 106

The Habeas Corpus, no. **86,** 184
Halsey, R. T. H., 5, 6, 11 n. 6, 63
Hampden, Richard, 46
Hanover, 49
Hanoverian forces, 22
Harris, John, 122, 124
Havana, 11 n. 4, 15
Hedges, Edward, 126
Hessian forces, 24, 27
[*Het Tegenwoordig Verward Europa*], no. **68,** 148
Hill, Draper, *Mr. Gillray The Caricaturist*, 118, 174 n. 1
THE HISTORICAL PAINTER, no. **99,** 211
Holland: symbolized as boar, 16; dog, 162, 180, 202; lion, 136, 138, 145, 146, 150; male (usually merchant), 15, 43, 94, 108, 116, 118, 120, 122, 130, 136, 140, 142, 145, 146, 148, 150, 152, 154, 158, 160, 166, 174, 176, 178, 190, 194, 198, 208; sailor, 150, 154
Hogarth, William, 2, 10 n. 3, 11 n. 5, 188 n. 1
Holland, Henry Fox, 1st baron, 27, 50, 52, 56, 122
The HORRORS of WAR a VISION, no. **88,** 188
Howard, Henry, 30
Howe, Gen. Sir George, 89
Howe, Adm. Richard, 4th viscount, 96
Howe, Gen. Sir William, 20, 96
Humphrey, Hannah, 132
Humphrey, William, 116, 118, 120, 122, 132 n. 1, 168, 170, 178, 186, 190, 198, 205
Hungary, 49
Hutchinson, Gov. Thomas, 8

India: symbolized as wheels, 52
Intolerable Acts, 78
Ireland, 49, 200, 212; symbolized as Hibernia, 116, 190; male, 130; wheels, 52

Jamaica, 49, 162

Jersey Islands, 116, 152, 162
JOHN BULL TRIUMPHANT, no. **54,** 120
Johnstone, Commo. (Governor) George, 96, 98, 112
Jones, I., 165
Jones, J., 30
Jones, John Paul, 140
Jonson, Ben: *Everyman in his own Humor*, 183; *Sejanus*, 36 n. 2
Juillet, J., 134
June, John, 20
Justice, 156

Katerfelto, Gustavus, 186
Kennett, lord mayor Brackley, 132
Keppel, Adm. Augustus, 115, 174, 178, 186
King George's War. *See* War of the Austrian Succession

Langham, John, 186
Laurie & Whittle, 103
Law, John: Mississippi Scheme, 2
Lee, Gen. Charles, 105
Liberty, Miss, 45, 46, 52, 74, 89, 110, 145, 146
Liberty Tree, 67, 69
LIBERTY TRIUMPHANT, no. **31,** 74
London Magazine, 8, 16, 28, 45, 54, 56, 70, 89
Long Island, 89
LOON NA. WERK 1780, no. **64,** 140
The LOSS of EDEN, no. **100,** 212
Louisbourg, 20, 28, 69 n. 2
Luther, Martin, 1

McAdam, Joseph, 5
McCrea, Jane, 93
Macaronies, 63, 65, 87, 90
The Machine to go without Asses, no. **20,** 52
Madras, 49
Malcomb, John, 65, 67, 69
Manila, 11 n. 4, 50
Mansfield, William Murray, 1st earl of, 8, 52, 72, 82, 89, 93, 120, 130, 162, 174
Maria Theresa, queen of Hungary, 49

REBELLION AND RECONCILIATION: SATIRICAL PRINTS ON THE REVOLUTION AT WILLIAMSBURG was composed in Caledonia type by Coghill Composition Company, Richmond, Virginia, and printed in photo-offset lithography by the Meriden Gravure Company, Meriden, Connecticut, on Mohawk Superfine paper. Binding was done by Haddon Craftsmen, Inc., Scranton, Pennsylvania. Hans E. Lorenz and Delmore A. Wenzel did the photography, and the book was designed by Richard Stinely.